The Essential Guide to
WOOD PALLET
PROJECTS

Stunning Ideas for
Furniture, Decor, and More

Samantha Hartman and Danny Darke

Skyhorse Publishing

Previously published as *Wood Pallet Workshop* (ISBN: 978-1-5107-0527-2)
and *Wood Pallet Wonders* (ISBN: 978-1-5107-2782-3).

Skyhorse books may be purchased in bulk at special discounts for sales
promotion, corporate gifts, fund-raising, or educational purposes. Special
editions can also be created to specifications. For details, contact the Special
Sales Department, Skyhorse Publishing, 307 West 36th Street, 11th Floor,
New York, NY 10018 or info@skyhorsepublishing.com.

Skyhorse® and Skyhorse Publishing® are registered trademarks
of Skyhorse Publishing, Inc.®, a Delaware corporation.

Visit our website at www.skyhorsepublishing.com.

10 9 8 7 6 5 4 3 2 1

Library of Congress Cataloging-in-Publication Data is available on file.

Photography on pages V–123 by Samantha Hartman and pages 124–256 by Danny Darke
Cover photos by Samantha Hartman and Danny Darke
Cover design by Kai Texel

Print ISBN: 978-1-5107-7966-2
Ebook ISBN: 978-1-5107-7972-3

Printed in China

CONTENTS

INTRODUCTION

Part of the charm of working with pallets is that they are imperfect. After being used and reused, all boards are not necessarily created equal, thereby giving you, the designer, freedom to create outside the bounds of perfection. Pallet projects usually have a personalized, non-conforming look to them, in a word: unique. Wood pallets give people of any skill level the opportunity to transform unused and unwanted materials into something of value, artistic or practical. Reinventing an old pallet is a great way to recycle unwanted material that would otherwise be thrown away, so you're helping the environment while also being savvy by not spending too much (or any) money.

Before you get started, there are a couple of things you should know that will make your life easier. In this book, you will learn simple ways to use pallets to create a variety of items, from basic shelves and serving trays to larger furniture, such as an industrial-style coffee table and a rustic headboard. With upcy-

cling old furniture, one would usually have to scavenge weekly garbage routes hoping to find the right item or pay for it at a yard sale or online, but pallets are free, consistently available, and come in different shapes and sizes, allowing anyone to pick one out and imagine it as something else, regardless of skill level. Try to create in the simplest, least expensive way possible while still making quality pieces that will last. All of the projects shown can be made with common tools that you likely have or can easily access.

CHAPTER ONE

GETTING STARTED WITH WOOD PALLETS

Variations of Pallets

Pallets come in a variety of forms. The first thing to look for in a pallet is whether it has lots of deck boards or slats and to make sure they are not warped. The more boards that match from a single pallet, the better they are for making furniture. The two most common types you will likely come across are stringer and block pallets. Other pallets that make appearances are wing pallets, boarded pallets, plywood pallets, skids, and hybrids.

Stringer Pallets

A stringer design is a pallet that has "stringers," or long pieces of wood, that run the length of the pallet and sit in between the top deck boards and the bottom deck boards. Stringers are often preferable over block pallets because they are lighter and easier to dismantle. Cutting a deck board off a block is not fun. That being said, they definitely have their place: block pallets are generally stronger and the boards are less likely to be damaged.

Block Pallets

A block design is a pallet that has a thick rectangular or square "block" that creates space between the top and bottom deck boards. There are usually four blocks—one in each corner, as well as one spaced between each corner, for a total of eight. However, they are all kinds of shapes and sizes. This is because there are also recycled pallets that have been either repaired for further use or manufactured out of recycled materials, so you never know what kind of monstrosities you could find with one of those.

Wing Pallets

Another type of pallet you may come across fairly often is a wing pallet. They are similar to a stringer with the most noticeable difference being that the deck boards extend longer past the stringer board giving it a "winged" look.

Boarded Pallets

The close-boarded pallet can have stringer boards or blocks between deck boards. They can be extremely heavy but make the best coffee tables, benches, and desks because they are smooth, sturdy, and usually even, giving you a leg up when building a piece of furniture that you need to be flush. Boarded pallets have boards placed right next to each other with no space between.

Plywood Pallets and Skids

Plywood pallets have—you guessed it—a piece of plywood in place of deck boards either on one or both sides. These pallets tend to be weird, and they are usually terribly warped or moldy, so they are generally not recommended. A skid is a mix between a close-boarded pallet and a wing pallet but with no bottom deck boards.

Hybrids

The term "hybrid" is used in a range of ways in connection to pallets, but it is used here to describe a pallet that does not easily fit into previously mentioned categories. Hybrids are pallets that subscribe to no particular form or shape and are created out of necessity, possibly missing pieces, and appearing in odd shapes or wood combinations. These pallets are extremely useful although unreliable to find as you never know what to expect.

Designing a project around a hybrid pallet can inspire you to think in a new direction. As an example, the pallet for the Coffee Table in this book is similar to a block or close-boarded pallet, but it only has four blocks and no bottom deck boards, so we can technically call it a hybrid. Another gem was the top of the Bar included in this book. It could have looked much different, but as it was found, it was perfect for the project. It may be a good idea to look for pallets from time to time before settling on a design because you never know what you might find.

Hopefully this information will help steer you in the right direction when picking which pallets to take home. On a bad day, you might end up dismantling four different pallets just to get enough good pieces to build one shelf. It is so much easier to pick the right pallets to begin with!

Treated Pallets vs. Untreated Pallets

Realistically, there is no sure way to be certain that the pallet you are working with is "safe" outside of going directly to the manufacturer and getting one fresh out of the oven. Any one who is picking up used pallets will not know exactly where and what such a pallet has been exposed to. Even if the person who provides you their leftover materials tells you where they come from and what they are used for—you are still just taking their word for it. However, do not let this news discourage you. You are not leading a dangerous life now because you have decided to craft with recycled materials. As with most things in life, a little common sense can guide you to safely selecting pallets.

Treated Pallets

Pallets that are marked or stamped with information tell you that it is used for export and has been treated according to the standards required by the country it was being shipped to. There are basically three different abbreviations you may come across on these stamps that will give you an indication of how a pallet—at some point in its past—was treated.

HT = Heat Treated
KD = Kiln Dried
MB = Methyl Bromide

(A fourth abbreviation people ask about is DB which stands for "debarked," but this one has nothing to do with the way it is treated in connection to your health.)

A quick glance at the above treatments without any further explanation is probably enough for it to become obvious which one you should pass on. Methyl-bromide treated pallets are not commonly found anymore but may show up in older stacks of wood. To give you perspective, this pesticide is also largely used as a soil fumigant in tomato, strawberry, grape, pepper, and other popular crops. You are possibly getting some methyl-bromide whether you choose to or not, so why not avoid adding more to your daily dose by passing on using MB-stamped pallets.

Untreated Pallets

An unmarked pallet may indicate that it was not treated because it is meant for domestic use and therefore never had to meet the standards of any other countries. Although these could be considered a safer bet, you still do not know which hazardous items they may have been used to transport.

The bottom line is as long as you try to select pallets that do not have dark, greasy spills of an unknown substance on them, do not smell strongly of chemicals, are not covered in mold or marked MB—you should be on the safe side. You will not be burning these pallets, releasing their chemicals into the air to inhale, and if you're like me, you are going to slather them in polyurethane anyway, thereby trapping any hidden toxins within.

Where to Find Pallets

Wood pallets are easily accessible items that can be found almost anywhere. Businesses such as grocery stores, hardware stores, and lumberyards often have them lying around and are happy to give them away for free. Construction companies and businesses often have items shipped in crates. Make sure you ask first just to be sure; sometimes pallets are sent back to the companies they came from.

It really is true that one man's trash is another man's treasure. You can check the local classified ads and Craigslist or ask friends and family. Use your imagination! It doesn't hurt to ask around, because you never know where you'll find them.

Pallet Safety

If you are working out of your home or garage, you will have to improvise as your space likely does not meet O.S.H.A. safety standards. Here are some tips to consider:

- Wear safety glasses when sanding or making cuts.
- Heavy work gloves are also a good item to keep around. When you're collecting pallets, gloves will protect your hands from splinters, nails, and any sharp edges where boards are cracked or rough.
- When using power tools, remember to always keep your fingers clear of the blade and use a push stick on the table saw for narrow boards.
- Be careful when lifting pallets by yourself and try not to lift them higher than chest level, for instance, when you are loading or unloading pallets from your car or truck.
- Be conscious of where all power tool cords are so as not to trip over them or have a cord get caught up short, causing your reciprocating saw to go flying out of your hands.
- Work in an area that has good ventilation.
- Pick up after yourself! You may forget about that rusty nail you removed that is now in your foot.
- If you are using a corded drill, be mindful of how powerful they are, as well as how scorching hot the screws can become when removing them with your drill.
- Do not work in bare feet or flip-flops; wear real shoes.
- If you are trying to screw into a board and the screw is making no progress, take the time to stop and drill a hole first instead of pushing as hard as you can.
- The closest calls will probably be when disassembling pallets with your reciprocating saw. Just make sure the wood you are cutting into is secured. If the entire pallet is shaking and vibrating loudly and you are having a hard time holding onto your saw, this is not a good sign, and something bad is about to happen.
- Do not stick your saw somewhere low on the pallet and start cutting up towards your face, and the same goes for cutting down towards your feet. Get your body out of the direction where the blade is headed when you are applying pressure to move the saw through the wood; once free, it might pop out and get you.
- If some of the tools in this book are new, be sure to practice with them until they feel comfortable. Don't be afraid to ask someone for a demonstration, whether it be a family member, a friend, or the person working at the tool-rental area of a hardware store.

By keeping these suggestions in mind and making sure you are familiar with all of your tools before using them, you will probably be all right!

Pallet Basics

Working with pallets is fairly straightforward, but there are a few things that are good to know to save yourself time.

Disassembling wood pallets is fastest, cleanest, and easiest on your body when tackled using a reciprocating saw. Be sure to fit it with a bi-metal blade that will work for metal and wood. The saw will cut right through your nail-embedded pallets. The downside to sawing off nails is that it will leave a small amount of the nail remaining in the board with a sharp edge that will need to be hammered down before sanding, or it will tear your sandpaper to shreds. If you decide to disassemble with a hammer and crow bar, get ready to sweat and be careful not to force the board off before you have loosened it enough to remove with ease. This can cause your board to break, rendering it useless and putting you back at square one. Heat-treated (HT) pallets split more easily, so be especially careful if you are using a crowbar on those.

Pallet-Making Tools, Materials, and Equipment

* Miter saw
* Reciprocating saw
* Jigsaw
* Hammer
* Sander
* Tape measure
* Nail gun
* Pencil
* Disposable paintbrushes
* Polyurethane
* Multipurpose screws
* Various sized nails
* Corded electric drill
* Wood glue
* Countersink drill bit

Using multipurpose screws over another type, such as wood screws, is highly recommended. They are tougher and grab the wood better. A countersink drill bit is also a good tool to have. It drills a cone-shaped hole into your board, allowing the screw to sit below the surface of your board, giving you a flush finish. Disposable paintbrushes are inexpensive chip brushes that you can find at hardware or department stores for around a dollar. They are the way to go since a lot of the time you will be painting with stain, which is a waste of energy trying to wash out of any brush. Better to throw them out and be done with the fumes. Finally, buy a corded drill over any cordless battery-operated type. Battery-operated drills are not powerful enough, have to be constantly charging, and the batteries can go bad. Then you can find yourself wondering if you grabbed the good battery or the bad one, and it just isn't worth the hassle. The cord is not a huge imposition, and this type of drill is much more powerful.

All of the projects in this book use wood pallets as the main material. Some of them use other unique materials, which are discussed in the next section, and some of them incorporate basic lumber from the hardware store. Each project will list which materials are needed for that piece, but be sure to read through the instructions beforehand.

Additional Tools and Materials

As you look through the projects in this book, you'll find that several of them use additional materials such as spindles, pieces of pipe, old windows, table legs, and branches. Using other reclaimed objects really brings character into a piece and makes it one of a kind. Although those things may not be as easy to come by as pallets, they are still there—you just have to know where to look. Visit your local antique shop, reclaimed building supply store, or even hardware store for ideas. If you have to buy something new, such as pipe, spray paint it or apply a patina to make it look old to match your project. Be sure to also check out thrift stores, estate and yard sales, flea markets, and Craigslist; if you don't find what you set out to, you might come home with something even better.

If you're using branches or logs, make sure they're well dried out. It's best to find them naturally. Cutting them fresh is not recommended because not only will this harm the tree, but the branches will take a long time to dry before you can use them.

Don't feel pressured to stick to the materials suggested in this book. If you find something else or want to reuse an object you have lying around the house, do it! Old pieces of barnwood, unique knobs or hooks, vintage wallpaper, or scraps of fabric can be incorporated to make a really beautiful piece.

Paint, Finish, and Sealing Materials

There are so many different ways to finish these projects that, no matter what look you're going for, you'll find it. For the most part, keeping wood as natural as possible looks great, so wax and wood stain are preferable over paint. These both come in a variety of colors. Keep a few small cans of each on hand. Before applying them to a project, brush a small square of each on a scrap pallet board to see how the wood takes the color.

For some projects, applying a lighter wax highlighted some of the unique markings, while a darker wax really made them pop. Make sure you read the drying time and instructions on each product, wear rubber gloves when applying them, and use them in a ventilated area.

For projects such as the Chevron Coffee Table and the Bar Cart, using a triple-thick polyurethane can really seal them well and make them water resistant. That can be applied with a paintbrush, and it works wonders to create a beautiful shine on a piece. Clear wax also works well for projects that you want to seal but not make super glossy.

There are a variety of different types of paint you can use, depending on the project. For some of the accents, such as the red cross on the Medicine Cabinet, standard acrylic paint from the craft store works well. The chalk paint used on projects such as the Knickknack Cubby Shelf and the outside of the Medicine Cabinet look great when distressed and sanded, and they add a nice texture as well.

On the Modern Bookshelf, you can get a color swatch at the hardware store and have them mix up a sample can. Those small cans are inexpensive, and they last a long time. For the Bar

Cart project, spray paint for the legs can give it a nice gold shine, while the rest utilizes chalk paint covered with lacquer.

Those are just a few ideas to get you started, but use whatever you think will work best for your project. On the pieces that use wallpaper or scrapbook paper for accents, a spray mount with a strong bond will work best. Using a vintage wallpaper on the back of the Modern Bookshelf or painting the lid boards of the Storage Chest in an ombre color would be a great way to finish either piece.

Workspace

Although a workshop is not needed for these projects, having a designated area for building is highly recommended. Sawdust is very fine and will cover everything! A folding table set up in the garage or out in the yard on a sunny day will work just fine.

Stay organized to make sure you don't mix up pieces or get glue all over the place. Use a lot of storage containers to hold tools, extra nails, and wood scraps. It's also important to keep the paint area separate from the cutting area to ensure dust doesn't stick to a wet project and ruin it.

CHAPTER TWO

MAKE YOUR HOUSE A HOME

CHEVRON COFFEE TABLE

If there's one project that you decide to leave with a natural finish, make it the Chevron Coffee Table. If you choose a pallet that varies in color and texture, you can create a really beautiful table simply through the weathering and history of the wood. The pallet I found had been sitting outside for a long time and the wood was old and brittle, but once I cleaned it up and put those final few coats of lacquer on the table, it easily turned into one of my favorite pieces in the book.

Tools

- Nail gun or hammer
- 1" nails
- 1½" nails
- Miter saw
- Wood glue
- Sandpaper
- Table saw
- Circular saw
- Ruler or square

Materials

- Pallet pieces
  Top (12): 8¼" × 3⅜"
  Trim (2): 2½" × ¾" × 8' boards (standard 1×3×8 from lumberyard)
- One 28¾" × 11⅛" piece of ⅝" plywood
- Four table legs

Instructions

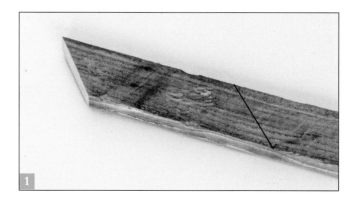

1. Take one of the 8¼" pieces and cut off both ends at a 45-degree angle, making sure that both angles face the same way to create a parallelogram shape. Repeat with the remaining 11 pieces.

2. Lay the boards out on the piece of plywood in a chevron shape, lining them up in the middle. They will overhang on each end.

3. Once you have the pieces arranged in a pattern you like, lift them up one at a time and apply wood glue underneath. Nail the corners of each board with 1" nails for extra support. Let dry.

4. Flip the piece over and carefully cut along the plywood on the two short ends to cut off the boards that are hanging over. You can use a jigsaw, bandsaw, or circular saw for this, whichever you're most comfortable with. Flip the piece back over.

5. Take the extra pieces cut off in Step 4 and fit them into the two empty spots on the top and bottom of the table. The pieces will go on the end opposite to the one they were cut from. Glue and nail into place.

6. Since I used a really old pallet for my project, the texture of the boards was varied and the edges needed trimming. Should that happen to you, flip the piece over and use a ruler or square to draw a straight line, then use the circular saw to trim along the plywood edge and even out the edges.

7. Measure each side of the table and add the width of the trim (¾"). Cut four pieces from the trim boards, two short and two long, and sand them smooth. If you choose to finish them in a different color than the table, do so now; it's easier to paint or stain them before attaching.

8. Once the trim is dry, take one of the long pieces and place it on one long edge of the table. Line one end up flush so it overhangs ¾" on the other end, and measure ½" from the top so there's a lip around the table top. It may be tricky to hold all those things in place at once, so I found this to be easiest: line the edges up flush and measure down ½" on the end, inserting a 1½" nail to tack the board in place. Then you can move down to the other end, measure down ½", and insert another nail while the other side is stabilized. Glue and nail the rest of the trim in place.

9. Repeat Step 8 with the other three trim pieces, moving around the edges and lining the ends up until it's all in place.

10. Flip the piece over and attach a leg plate to each corner using the included hardware. Check to make sure the included screws aren't too long; if they are you'll need to provide your own. Screw in the legs.

11. Finish the table with a few coats of lacquer for a water-resistant surface and to preserve the characteristics of the wood.

RUSTIC NIGHTSTAND

When refurbishing a spare bedroom, I found that the furniture I had on hand didn't fit the room—the look was off, the pieces were too big, and it just didn't feel complete. Rather than spend hours searching for something that would work, I decided to build my own, and the Rustic Nightstand was born. Although small in size, this piece has tons of storage space, with a drawer for holding smaller items and a bottom shelf that's perfect for an extra blanket or a basket of books. Whether you finish it to match a dresser you already have or leave it natural, it's sure to complement the rest of the room and act as a functional piece of furniture.

Tools

- Nail gun or hammer
- ¾" nails
- 1" nails
- 1½" nails
- Miter saw
- Wood glue
- Sandpaper
- Table saw
- Drill
- Drill bit one size smaller than the drawer pull
- Ruler or square
- Level

Materials

- Pallet pieces
  Shelves (12): 15½" × 3½"
  Sides (8): 25" × 4"
  Front trim (3): 14" × 1"
  Back (1): 14" × 3¾"
  Braces (6): 14" × 1½"
  Drawer front and back (2): 13½" × 3"
  Drawer sides (2): 14" × 3"
- One 13½" × 15" piece of lauan plywood
- Drawer pull

1. Take four of the shelf pieces and lay them out to form the top of the nightstand, with the good sides down. Lay one brace piece on each end to hold the top pieces together and secure in place with glue and ¾" nails. Repeat with the remaining shelf and brace pieces to form three shelves. Sand smooth.

2. To attach the sides to the top of the nightstand, line one of the side boards up with the top edge of one of the shelves created in Step 1, making sure it's flush with the side and top of one of the brace pieces. Glue and nail in place with 1½" nails. Attach three more side pieces along the edge, leaving a ½" overhang on the front. Repeat with the other side of the nightstand, making sure the overhang is facing in the same direction.

3. On the back of the nightstand, attach the back piece under the top shelf, securing it in place from the top and sides with glue and 1½" nails.

4. Flip the piece over so it's sitting upside down and insert another one of the shelves. Be sure the brace pieces are flush with the back piece inserted in Step 3. Tack the back two corners in place with two nails from the outside to make the shelf easier to work with. Use a level to make sure the shelf is level and use nails to attach it firmly in place.

5. Use the ruler or square to mark off along the sides where the nails should go to make it easier to attach, and secure all around with glue and 1½" nails.

6. Measure 2½" from the bottom of each inside corner to find the placement for the bottom shelf. Place the shelf on the outside of each line and attach it in place with nails, making sure it's flush with the back of the nightstand and the brace pieces are against the sides.

7

7.   Turn the nightstand with the front facing forward. Attach a front trim piece on each shelf to cover the raw edges.

8

8.   To create the drawer, lay out the front, back, and side pieces to form a box and secure them with wood glue and 1½" nails, making sure the front and back boards are on the outside of the two shorter sides.

9. Attach the piece of lauan to the bottom by gluing around the edges and nailing in place with 1½" nails.

10. Use a ruler to find the center of the front of the drawer. Pre-drill the hole using a drill bit that is one size smaller than the drawer pull.

11. Sand the nightstand smooth and finish it with your choice of paint or stain. I left mine natural, without any sealant, to show off the color of the wood. Attach and secure the drawer pull.

MODERN BOOKSHELF

When visualizing this piece, I wanted to create something with clean lines, yet with a surprise element to draw attention to it. Using a set of Midcentury Modern legs I found at a reclaimed building supply store as a source of inspiration helped me to do just that. Painting the legs and the accent lines on the shelf in the same color will make this piece tie in easily with any room or really stand on its own and become a topic of conversation.

Tools

- Nail gun or hammer
- ¾" nails
- 1½" nails
- ⅜" screws
- Miter saw
- Wood glue
- Sandpaper
- Table saw

Materials

- Pallet pieces
  Back and sides (11): 26" × 4½" × ½"
  Top and bottom (6): 22½" × 4⅝"
  Back strips (4): 22½" × 1½"
  Side strips (8): 14" × 1½"
  Shelf (3): 21¼" × 4½"
  Shelf braces (2): 13" × 1½"
- Four 2" metal corner brace brackets
- Four table legs

Instructions

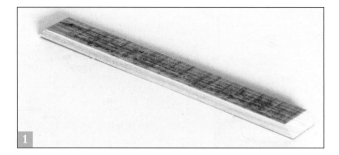

1. Take the back and side strips and place each one in the miter saw with the 1½" side standing up. Cut each end off at a 45-degree angle, making the two cuts face each other to give each board a short top edge and a long bottom edge. Set aside.

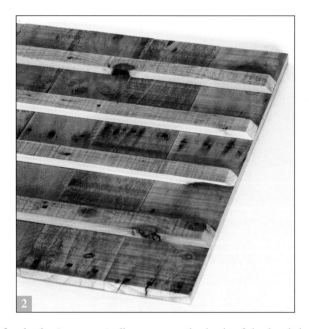

2. Lay out the five back pieces vertically to create the back of the bookshelf. Measure in 4" from each short side and make a mark. Place a back strip on the inside of each mark with the long bottom edge face down. Measure 4" toward the center from those two pieces and place the two remaining back strips. There should be four evenly spaced boards laid across, 4" from each edge and with 4" between each piece. Secure in place using glue and ¾" nails.

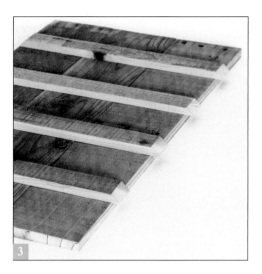

3. Lay out three of the side boards and four side strips as in Step 2, lining the strips up flush with one side. They should hang over the other side by ½" to create a lip. Secure in place with glue and ¾" nails. Repeat with the remaining side pieces to create the other side of the bookshelf.

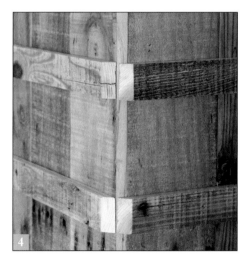

4. Line up one of the side pieces with the back piece, using the overhang from the side piece to create a lip over the back piece. Secure in place with glue and 1½" nails.

5. Connect the other side of the bookshelf in the same way, and then connect the two halves to form the shape of the bookshelf.

6. Take three of the top pieces and lay them across the top of the bookshelf. Attach with glue and 1½" nails. Flip the piece over and repeat with the three bottom pieces.

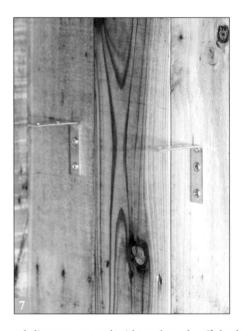

7. Measure down an equal distance on each side and mark off the location of the shelf. You may wish to place it in the center, off-center to create spaces for smaller and larger books, or add more than one shelf for a variety of items. Attach the metal brackets with ⅜" screws.

8. For the shelf, lay the three shelf boards out and measure over 3" from each short end. Mark a line and lay the two brace pieces on the inside of each line. Attach with glue and ¾" nails.

9. Attach the table legs to the bottom corners of the bookshelf frame using the screws included with the bracket.

10. Insert the shelf inside the bookshelf on top of the brackets.

BAR CART

I wanted to create a few projects that one would never imagine building out of wood, and the Bar Cart is just that. However, I still wanted to create a piece with a high-end look to it, so I painted the cart gold and white and finished it with a few coats of glossy lacquer to make it appear more modern. If you choose to attach a handle, some ideas include a bathroom towel rod, building one from wood, or using a dowel rod held in place with unique hooks.

Tools

- Nail gun or hammer
- 1" nails
- 1½" nails
- Miter saw
- Wood glue
- Sandpaper
- Table saw
- Bandsaw or jigsaw
- Phillips screwdriver or drill

Materials

- Pallet pieces
  Legs (8): 28" × 1½"
  Front and back (2): 20" × 4" × ½"
  Sides (2): 16" × 4" × ½"
  Insides (10): 15" × 4"
  Braces (4): 18" × 1½"
- Casters
- Handle (optional)

1. Take two of the 28" leg pieces and lay them out in an L shape. Secure together with glue and 1" nails, noting that there is a long edge and short edge to each leg.

2. Repeat with the remaining pieces to create four legs.

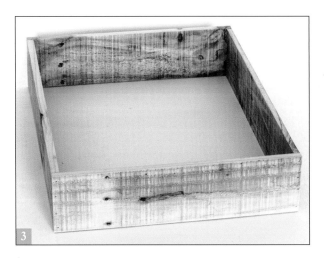

3. Lay out the front, back, and side pieces to form a box and attach with glue and 1½" nails, making sure the long boards are on the outside of the two shorter sides.

4. Take five of the inside pieces and lay them out to form the inside of the tray. Measure 3" toward the center from one side and secure a brace piece in place with glue and ¾" nails. Repeat with another brace on the opposite side.

5. Repeat Step 4 with the remaining five inside pieces and two braces to create the bottom shelf of the cart.

6. Take the shelf created in Step 5 and lay it face down. Take one of the legs and stand it up in one of the corners, making sure the long edge of the leg is facing the long side of the shelf. Trace around it using a pencil and repeat for the other corners, paying careful attention to the way the edges face.

7. Use a bandsaw or jigsaw to cut out the four corners along the lines created in Step 6 and sand smooth. Test fit the legs to make sure they sit flush with the shelf.

8. Sand all of the pieces smooth, paint them, and let them dry. It's easier to finish the pieces before assembly because of the way they're put together.

9. Take the sides of the cart tray from Step 3 and measure down 1½" from each corner, making a mark on the inside. Secure the legs in place with glue and ¾" nails, matching up the long edges with the long sides. Repeat with the other three legs.

10. Set the inside of the tray in place with the braces face down. Carefully nail it in place along the corners, shooting in a few 1½" nails from the top.

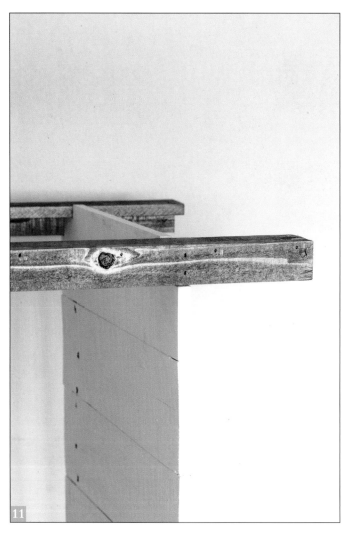

11. Measure up 5" from the bottom of each leg and make a mark. Hold the bottom shelf in place and attach each corner, nailing into the notches with the 1½" nails.

12. To finish, screw a caster to the bottom of each leg and attach a handle to one short side of the tray part of the cart (if you choose to do so). Seal with a few coats of lacquer to make it water resistant.

HERB GARDEN

Simple and rustic, this Herb Garden really shows off the beautiful color and vibrant life of whatever herbs or flowers you choose to plant in it. Because my planter was to be used on the porch, I opted not to paint the piece and selected old and very weathered pallets for the legs. I really wanted to create a piece that would work well in a small space yet still hold a lot of plants. You can modify this planter with longer shelves, more shelves, or smaller pots to hold more plants.

Tools

- Nail gun or hammer
- 1½" nails
- Miter saw
- Wood glue
- Sandpaper
- Drill or drill press
- 3" hole saw blade
- Jigsaw (optional)

Materials

- Pallet pieces
  Legs (4): 43" × 3¼" × 1½"
  Shelves (3): 26" × 4½" (can be any width but at least 4½")
  Braces (12): 3" × 1½" × ¾"
- Nine 3½" terra cotta pots

1. Remove any remaining nails from the leg pieces and sand smooth. Lay one out with the wider edge facing up and set the other three aside.

2. Measure 4", 18", and 32" from one side, marking off each. Place a brace piece on each mark with the wider edge face up, on the side of the line closest to where you measured from. Attach each piece in place with glue and 1½" nails. Repeat with the other three legs.

3. Take one of the shelves and mark off the center. Measure over 5½" in each direction and make a mark. Using a drill, or a drill press with the hole saw blade, drill out the three holes to create the spaces where the pots will go, centering the drill bit over the marks. (A jigsaw may also be used if a hole saw is not available. Simply draw a 3" circle, drill a small hole to insert the jigsaw blade, and cut out.)

4. Repeat Step 3 with one more of the shelves.

5. Take one of the shelves with the holes and measure over 1" from each side. Set the shelf on the top brace of one leg, lining up the 1½" mark with the edge of the leg to create an overhang. Nail in from the top of the shelf. Repeat this process with the remaining three legs on the other sides of the shelf.

6

6. Repeat Step 5 to nail the other two shelves in place, keeping in mind that the shelf with no holes goes on the bottom. I chose to use pots with drainage holes in them so when I water the top plants, the water will drip down into the next ones. Using a bottom shelf with no holes will create space for saucers to sit so the water won't drip onto the floor. If you chose pots without drainage holes, you may drill holes in all three shelves because the water won't drip out.

7. You may also use narrow strips of wood, pieces of twine, or even thin branches to create a fence around the bottom shelf to hold the pots in place. I love the look of terra cotta so I chose to leave mine open, but another natural element would look great across the bottom.

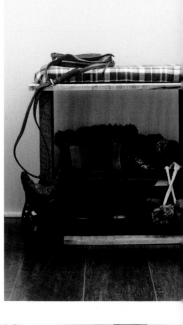

CHAPTER THREE

STAY ORGANIZED

HAT RACK

For most of the projects in this book, wood pallets are disassembled and reused in ways that hide their original purpose. However, the Hat Rack uses a whole pallet to create a unique and useful bedroom accessory for displaying hats, scarves, belts, jewelry, or purses. Hooks may be added to the boards on the front for additional items, and using a larger pallet will add extra "shelves" to the piece.

Tools

- Hammer
- 1½"–2" nails
- Reciprocating saw, jigsaw, or circular saw
- Sandpaper
- Yardstick or 3' level for drawing a long line

Materials

- Whole pallet
- Sturdy hook for hanging

1. Begin this project by choosing a pallet with good bones. The boards should be free of cracks and nails, and a sturdy center brace is essential for hanging.

2. Stand the pallet up with the boards running horizontally. Use the yardstick or long level to draw a line from one top corner down to the bottom center. Repeat on the other side to create a downward-facing arrow shape.

3. Using a reciprocating saw, jigsaw, or circular saw, cut along the lines on the front of the pallet. Any of those tools will work fine; choose the one that will work best with the shape and size of your pallet.

4. Remove the boards from the back of the pallet and trim the center brace where you want the top and bottom of the rack to be. Sand smooth.

5. Hammer a few additional nails into the center brace where the boards cross for added stability. Attach a sturdy hook on the back, and because this piece is heavy, be sure to mount it in a stud.

SHABBY CHIC TOOLBOX

The Shabby Chic Toolbox is one of my favorite projects. It's super-versatile and can be used in so many ways, from storing kitchen utensils and organizing art supplies to showing off holiday décor and making a home for your favorite plants. Not only can it be finished in any color, but the handle really makes it stand out from the crowd. I used a thick branch for my project to bring some of the outdoors in. If you're after a more modern look, a piece of copper pipe would look great with a navy blue painted box.

Tools

- Nail gun or hammer
- 1½" nails
- Miter saw
- Wood glue
- Sandpaper
- Table saw
- Jigsaw
- Two 2" screws
- Drill with drill bit that is one size narrower than your screws
- Glass or similar object 2" in diameter for tracing
- Marking pencil

Materials

- Five pallet boards at least 17" long
- Something unique for the handle, such as a thick branch, dowel rod, piece of pipe, or spindle

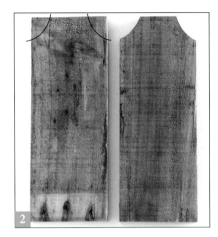

1. Measure and cut two boards to a length of 17" and two to 12". The 12" boards will be placed vertically to form the ends of the toolbox.

2. On the top corners of each of the 12" boards, draw two symmetrical arcs using the glass or other object as a pattern. Cut along the lines with a jigsaw. Sand all four pieces, making sure the curves on the end pieces are smooth.

3. Lay out the four boards to form a box, making sure the long boards for the sides line up on the outside of the two ends. Apply glue where the boards meet, then nail the boards together.

4. Using a table saw, rip the last board down into three 1½"-wide strips. Cut each strip to a length of 17", then sand until smooth.

5. Attach the strips to the bottom of the toolbox using glue; the edges should be flush with the sides. Carefully nail all around the outside of the box.

6. Measure the inside distance between the two tall ends of the toolbox and cut the handle to that length. Measure an equal distance down on each end and mark where you want to place the handle. Hold the handle in place and pre-drill two holes. If you chose something such as a dowel rod or piece of pipe, use a paddle bit that is the width of the handle to create two holes to slide it into.

7. Paint the toolbox with a finish of your choosing. I painted mine with two coats of white paint and then sanded down some of the edges to create a distressed look. If your handle needs painting, do that now as well. The handle I chose for the box was a thick branch, so I used a light brown wax to highlight its character and make it smooth to the touch.

8. Once everything is dry, use the two screws to attach the handle.

WOODEN CRATE

One of the most versatile projects in the book, this Wooden Crate can be customized to any size to allow for a variety of uses. Set them on the floor to hold blankets or dog toys, or use them in conjunction with another project such as the Storage Bench to hold shoes or winter accessories. These instructions result in a crate that's 16" × 12" × 8" when finished, but it can be altered by shortening or lengthening the sides. This project is great for using up some of the scraps left over from others, and I found I didn't have to rip down very many boards after digging through my bin of leftovers.

Tools

- Nail gun or hammer
- 1½" nails
- Miter saw
- Wood glue
- Sandpaper
- Table saw

Materials

- Pallet pieces
  Scraps (4): 1" × 2" × 8"
  Sides (8): 12" × 1½"
  Sides (8): 16" × 1½"
  Bottom (5): 12" × 1½"
  Bottom (2): 12" × 4½"

Instructions

1. Cut the boards to the listed sizes. Sand them smooth and paint, stain, or wax them, if you choose to finish this piece. Let dry.

2. Take one of the 1" × 2" × 8" scraps. Lay it on a short side and attach four of the 16" boards with a bit of wood glue and nails, spaced out evenly.

5

3. Repeat with the other end of the boards, attaching the strips to another one of the scraps.

4. Repeat Steps 3 and 4 with the remaining 16" strips.

5. Take one of the completed sides and attach four of the 12" strips. Repeat with the other completed side.

6. Attach the two halves together, gluing and nailing any remaining strips.

7. Spread a line of glue over the top edge and attach the bottom pieces with nails, alternating the various widths in an appealing pattern.

STORAGE CHEST

Although the Storage Chest is one of the larger projects in the book, don't be fooled into thinking it's one of the more difficult. Perfect for a children's room or storing away gardening supplies for winter, this chest can be customized to fit any theme or style. For example, a nautical look can be achieved by painting the chest dark blue and drilling holes in the sides for knotted rope handles. You can finish the inside by cutting a few pieces of heavy cardboard ⅛" smaller than the dimensions of each side of the chest, covering one side of the cardboard with spray mount, and wrapping each piece in fabric. Use a staple gun to secure the cardboard pieces to the inside of the chest to give it a more polished look.

Tools

- Nail gun or hammer
- ¾" nails
- 1½" nails
- 3" nails
- ¾" screws
- Miter saw
- Wood glue
- Sandpaper
- Table saw
- Phillips screwdriver or drill
- Ruler

Materials

- Pallet pieces
  Sides (20): 20" × 4½"
  Bottom (5): 27" × 4"
  Lid (5): 27" × 4⅛"
  Braces (2): 16" × 1¼"
  Accents (4): 27" × 3"
  Accents (4): 20" × 3"
- Four metal gate brackets
- Two metal handles
- Two 2" metal hinges
- Casters (optional)

Instructions

1. Sand all pieces smooth.

2. Take one of the 27" accent boards and lay it out with the good side down. Place one of the side boards square with the corner of the accent piece, also with the good side facedown, and then glue and nail it in place with ¾" nails along the top and bottom of the accent board. Repeat with five more side boards, lining them up across the accent board.

3. Repeat Step 2 with the other 27" accent board and six more side boards. These will create the front and back of the chest.

4. The sides of the chest will be created in a similar fashion, using one 20" accent board and four side boards for each. However, the side boards will be centered on the accent piece, leaving 1" on each side to create a lip. Be sure that the bottom edges are flush, and then glue and nail in place. Repeat with the other side.

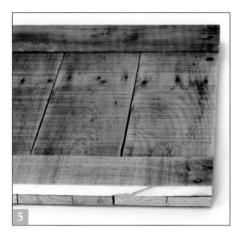

5. Take all four sides of the chest and repeat Steps 2 through 4, attaching another accent board to the top of each piece.

6. Now it's time to assemble the chest. Take the front and one of the side pieces and stand them up to form a corner. The 1" overhangs created in Step 4 will act as a lip to hold the pieces together more firmly. Carefully attach the two pieces together using glue and the 3" nails along the corners and the 1½" nails along the sides.

7. Repeat Step 6 with the back and remaining side to create the other half of the chest. Line up the two halves and nail them together to create a box.

8. Take the five 27" bottom pieces and lay them across the top of the box with the long edges lining up to create the bottom of the chest. Attach by carefully gluing and nailing all around the edges using 1½" nails. Set aside.

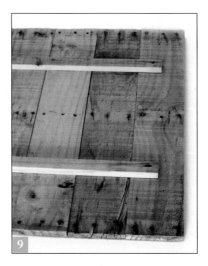

9. Lay out the five lid boards. Measure over 6" from each short side and draw a line all the way across. Place a 16" brace piece on the inside of each line and attach with glue and ¾" nails to hold it in place. Flip the lid over and reinforce the brace boards with ¾" screws across the top.

10. If you wish to paint or stain the chest, do so now. I finished mine using Rustic Pine wax to keep a lighter color and bring out the natural tones of the wood. Set aside to dry.

11. To attach the lid, measure over five inches from each side on the lid, and the same distance on the top edge of the chest. Use the screws that come with the hinge to attach it. Please note that you may need to use smaller screws on the lid so they don't come through the other side, depending on the size that comes with the hinge.

12. Attach the decorative gate brackets to the four front corners of the chest, and the handles to each side. You may also add casters to the four bottom corners of the chest.

STORAGE BENCH

For the Storage Bench, I wanted to create a piece that incorporated one of the Wooden Crates. Using thick pallet boards provides extra support and an interesting visual contrast when placed next to the thin dowel rods on the sides of the bench. When finished, this piece can be used by the front door to hold hats and gloves, in a spare bedroom to hold sheets, or in a children's room for shoes. This bench was built to hold a 16" × 12" × 8" crate but can be easily adjusted by altering the length and width of the top and bottom boards or the height of the legs.

Tools

- Nail gun or hammer
- 1" nails
- 1½" nails
- Miter saw
- Wood glue
- Sandpaper
- Table saw
- Drill or drill press
- ⅜" drill bit

Materials

- Pallet pieces
  Legs (4): 19" × 3½" × 1½"
  Braces (4): 8" × 1¾" × 1¼"
  Top and bottom (10): 24" × 3½"
- Eight 18½" × ⅜" dowel rods

Instructions

1. Take one of the brace pieces and mark off down the center of the board at 1", 3", 5", and 7". Be sure to position the board so the 1¼" edge is facing up. Drill all the way through the board at each mark using the ⅜" bit. Repeat with the other three brace pieces.

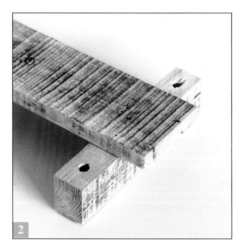

2. Center one of the 24" top pieces over one of the brace pieces in a T shape, with the top piece 1½" from the end. Glue and nail in place with 1" nails. Repeat with the other end of the top piece and another brace piece.

3. Attach two more 24" pieces to the top, one on each side of the center piece.

4. Repeat Steps 3 and 4 with the remaining two brace pieces and three 24" bottom pieces.

5. Take the finished top piece from Step 2 and position one of the legs next to the brace piece, being sure to turn it so the 3½" edge is facing out. Glue and nail in place using 1½" nails. Repeat for the other leg.

6. Attach the two legs on the other side in the same manner, forming all four legs of the bench.

7. Put a dowel rod into each hole, tapping them in with a hammer if needed to make sure they're snug. If you want them a different color than the bench, you can paint them during this step to make it easier than when the bench is fully assembled.

8. Take the bottom part of the bench and put it in place, carefully lining up all of the dowel rods in the holes.

9. Place two of the remaining 24" pieces on the top and two on the bottom, gluing and nailing them all in place on the legs with 1½" nails.

10. Paint or stain the bench in a color of your choice.

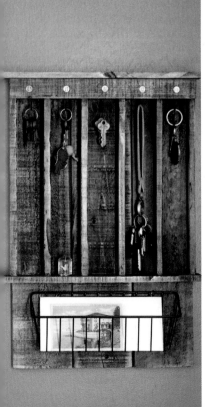

CHAPTER FOUR

ON THE WALL

PHOTO DISPLAY SHELF

The Photo Display Shelf is a small project that packs a huge punch. Leaving the piece unfinished shows off the true potential of wood pallets, but painting it a solid color makes it a great accent piece for a room. For my shelf braces, I used a scrap of old barnwood I'd been holding onto for a while. It was just the right size for this piece, full of the history and texture I was looking for, and it really complements the natural look of the pallet wood.

Tools

- Nail gun or hammer
- 1¼" nails
- Miter saw
- Wood glue
- Sandpaper
- Table saw

Materials

- Pallet pieces
  Back (3): 16" × 3¼"
  Shelf (1): 9¾" × 3¼"
- Two 9¾" pieces (can be a 1×1 or 1×2 from the lumberyard, or an interesting scrap of old wood)
- Clip, hook, clothespin, etc., for hanging photos

1. Lay out the three back pieces vertically and measure 3" from the top and bottom. Place the two brace pieces on the inside of those lines and glue and nail in place from the front.

2. Lay the shelf piece on top of the bottom brace and secure from the top with nails. Be sure to also add a few nails from the back.

3. Find a unique hook to hang photos. I attached one large decorative clothespin with hot glue for a simple shelf, but several mini clothespins would work well for holding multiple photos or mementos. A large binder clip would be great for holding a notepad for groceries, or a hook can be used to hang a small picture frame.

MEDICINE CABINET

I originally created this Medicine Cabinet as additional storage for a small bathroom, and you'll be surprised at how much you can stow away in it. It's perfect for holding not only vitamins and medicine but also makeup brushes or a decorative jar of cotton balls. This piece can easily be resized to insert more shelves, and could be finished in a high-gloss white for a modern look.

Tools

- Nail gun or hammer
- 1½" nails
- ¼" screws (16)
- Miter saw
- Wood glue
- Sandpaper
- Table saw

Materials

- Pallet pieces
  Sides (2): 16" × 4½"
  Sides (2): 12" × 4½"
  Shelf (1): 12" × 4½"
  Door (2): 12" × 1½"
  Door (2): 9" × 1½"
  Back (4): 12½" × 4"
- One 12" × 16" piece of lauan or thin plywood
- Handle or decorative knob
- Two 1" metal hinges
- Magnetic clasp (optional)

Instructions

1. Lay out the four sides to form a box and secure together with glue and nails, making sure the long boards are on the outside of the two shorter sides.

2. Measure down an equal distance inside the box on each long side for the shelf. I positioned mine a little higher up than center to allow room for larger jars on the bottom and smaller items on top. Attach using glue and 1½" nails, inserting them in from both sides.

3. Attach the four back boards across the back with glue and nails. Set aside.

4. Take one of the 12" pieces for the door and apply glue to one of the long faces. Lay the piece of plywood on top, lining up the long edges, and screw in place using four of the screws. Repeat with the other 12" piece, and then with the two 9" pieces for the top and bottom of the door.

5. Sand the cabinet smooth and paint it white. I left the inside of mine natural and distressed the door for a unique look. Paint a red cross on the front and let dry.

6. To finish, attach a handle or knob on the right side of the door. Attach the door to the cabinet with the hinges, measuring 3" from the top and bottom. You may also wish to add a magnetic clasp to the inside of the door to keep it shut.

KNICKKNACK CUBBY SHELF

When designing this project, I imagined a shelf that would be perfect in a rustic outdoor greenhouse, packed full of terra cotta pots, seed packets, and twine. In reality, I used this shelf in a guest bedroom to hold small trinkets but finished it in a way that would tie in with the space I created in my mind, using green chalk paint and a vintage floral wallpaper I'd picked up from an estate sale a few years ago.

Tools

- Nail gun
- 1½" nails
- Miter saw
- Wood glue
- Sandpaper
- Table saw

Materials

- Pallet pieces
  Sides (2): 24" × 4½"
  Sides (2): 12" × 4½"
  Shelves (1): 23" × 4"
  Shelves (6): 5¾" × 4"
  Front (4): 12" × 1¾"
- One piece of 12½" × 24" plywood
- Spray mount
- Wallpaper
- Sawtooth hanger

Instructions

1. Lay out the four sides to form a box and secure together with glue and nails, making sure the long boards are on the outside of the two shorter sides. Be sure to note the bottom board, which is 4" deep and sits ½" shallower than the other three sides.

2. Find the center of the two short sides of the box created in Step 1 and attach the 23" shelf board using glue and nails. Be sure the center shelf board is flush with the bottom of the box.

3. On each of the two long sides and the center shelf, divide the length up into quarters and mark off where the cross shelves will go. Attach all six shelves, gluing and nailing in from the outside.

4. Lay the four front pieces across the shelves to create the cubbies, making sure that the bottom piece is positioned at the bottom. Glue and then nail across the shelves, as well as in from the sides, to hold in place.

5. If you're going to paint the piece, do so now after sanding it smooth. Set aside to dry.

6. Take the piece of plywood for the back and spray it with spray mount. Let it dry around a minute until tacky and lay on a piece of wallpaper. Smooth out any wrinkles and press to adhere. Trim any excess paper from the edges and let dry.

7. Flip the cubby shelf over and attach the back, carefully gluing and nailing all around the exterior. Center a sawtooth hanger on the back for mounting.

FARMHOUSE SPICE RACK

After an unsuccessful search for the perfect spice rack for my kitchen, I decided to make one of my own. I kept the design relatively simple, and I love the way the vintage metal canisters and jars full of dry goods look against the natural finish of the pallet wood. The rack can also be used for other purposes around the house, such as displaying seashells from various trips, storing jars of buttons, or holding miscellaneous screws and nails.

Tools

- Nail gun or hammer
- 1½" nails
- Miter saw
- Wood glue
- Sandpaper
- Table saw
- Ruler or square

Materials

- 10 pallet boards at least 24" long
- Sawtooth hanger

ENTRYWAY KEY RACK

Inspired by old hotel-style key racks, this smaller version brings a bit of vintage charm to your home. Any type of basket can be used for the letter holder at the bottom. I picked up a simple closet storage basket from Target, cut off the wire hooks, and spray-painted it black. Not only does this work perfectly, but it fits the style of the piece as well.

Tools

- Nail gun or hammer
- 1½" nails
- Miter saw
- Wood glue
- Sandpaper
- Table saw
- Ruler

Materials

- Pallet pieces
  Top and bottom (2): 15¼" × 2½"
  Key slots (6): 13" × 1½"
  Key slot brace (2): 14¼" × 1½"
  Back (3): 22" × 4¾"
- Five hooks
- Five decorative numbers, such as scrap-booking brads
- Wire basket around 12" × 4"

1. Determine the size for your project. Cut six boards to the same length and set two aside. Lay out the remaining four boards and measure the distance across (measurement A). Measure the depth of two boards (measurement B). Subtract B from A and cut the remaining four boards to that length for the top, bottom, and two shelves. Lay everything out and see how it fits together, adjusting accordingly.

2. For my project, I wanted to put narrower spice jars on display, so I didn't make the rack too deep. I ripped the top, bottom, and shelving boards down to 3" using a table saw, but if you have larger items, such as mason jars, you would want to leave them wider. Sand the boards smooth.

3. Take two of the longer boards and two of the shorter boards, and then glue and nail them together, making the rectangular front of the rack. The shorter boards should be on the inside of the longer. Be sure to line up the nail gun straight with the board you are shooting into.

4. Flip the rectangle over and put a bead of glue all the way around. Lay the four back pieces on it and nail all around the outside.

5. Flip the piece over to the front. I put two shelves in mine, but you're free to add as many as you would like. Measure down equally on both sides and mark where they'll go. Place one shelf in and put a nail in each side to hold it in place. Use the ruler or square to make sure it's level, and then use it to lightly draw a line on the outside of the rack to line up the nails. Finish securing the shelf in place, and then repeat with the other shelf.

6. Once more, flip the whole piece back over. Using the ruler, connect the lines you drew in Step 5 across the back of the rack. This will give you the center of each shelf to help you to finish nailing it all together. The lines will easily sand off when you're finished.

7. Now that the assembly is finished, paint or stain the piece however you like. I chose to leave mine natural because I really liked the characteristics of the wood, so I just lightly sanded it with a finer-grit paper and installed a sawtooth hanger on the back for hanging.

ENTRYWAY KEY RACK

Inspired by old hotel-style key racks, this smaller version brings a bit of vintage charm to your home. Any type of basket can be used for the letter holder at the bottom. I picked up a simple closet storage basket from Target, cut off the wire hooks, and spray-painted it black. Not only does this work perfectly, but it fits the style of the piece as well.

Tools

- Nail gun or hammer
- 1½" nails
- Miter saw
- Wood glue
- Sandpaper
- Table saw
- Ruler

Materials

- Pallet pieces
  Top and bottom (2): 15¼" × 2½"
  Key slots (6): 13" × 1½"
  Key slot brace (2): 14¼" × 1½"
  Back (3): 22" × 4¾"
- Five hooks
- Five decorative numbers, such as scrapbooking brads
- Wire basket around 12" × 4"

Instructions

1. Sand all of the pieces smooth.

2. Lay the three back pieces next to each other. Take one of the 15¼" pieces for the top and stand it up on one of the short sides, lining it up with the top of the back pieces, leaving ½" on each side. Flip the whole thing over, and then glue and nail the top piece in place. Set aside.

3. Take the two key slot brace pieces and nail them together in the shape of an "L."

4. Take the piece from Step 3 and attach one of the 13" key slot strips to the end, keeping the piece square with the board it's being nailed into. Repeat for the other end.

5. Measure and mark where the four remaining 13" key slot strips go, evenly spacing them across the board from the last step. Attach with glue and nails.

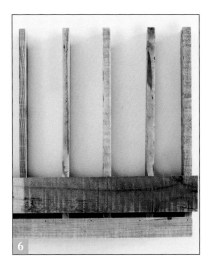

6. Take the 15¼" bottom piece and lay it across the six key slot boards. Mark off the center of each to indicate where to nail.

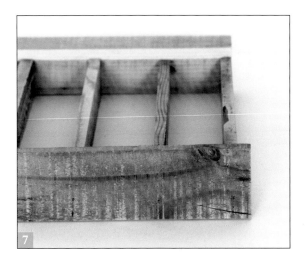

7. Attach the bottom piece, making sure both it and the key slot boards are flush with the table.

8. Place the piece from Step 7 on the back piece from Step 2, making sure the L-shaped piece is at the top. Flip it all over. Using the ruler, trace a line across the center of the bottom piece to show where to glue, nail, and attach.

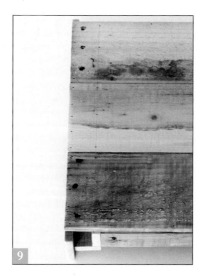

9. Do the same across the top, as well as shooting a few nails in through the top of the entire piece to hold it all together.

10. Finish the piece in the color of your choice. I used a Rustic Pine colored wax to highlight the natural tones of the wood. I spray-painted the hooks and basket black to match the number brads. Screw in the hooks, gently nail or superglue the numbers above the key slots, and attach the basket with wire, nails, or hooks, as appropriate.

CHAPTER FIVE

DECORATE YOUR SPACE

HEXAGON SHELF

A set of Hexagon Shelves is a great way to display your favorite knickknacks or tie together a gallery wall. The measurements in this project create a shelf that's about 13" across, but it can easily be adjusted to make different sizes. To figure it out, take your desired hexagon width and divide it in half to get the length of the cut sides (for example, for shelves that are 10" wide you would cut 5" long boards). It may vary slightly depending on how thick your pallets are, but that should give you a general idea. These shelves are easy enough to whip up in an afternoon, yet they look like they took hours to create.

Tools

- Nail gun or hammer
- 1½" nails
- Miter saw
- Wood glue
- Sandpaper
- Orbital sander

Materials

- Three pallet boards at least 20" long (this is more than needed to allow for nail heads in the boards or trimming off split edges)
- Sawtooth hanger

Instructions

1. Begin this project by setting your miter saw to a 30-degree angle. Be sure to note the size of your saw blade so you know what width boards you can cut. For example, the blade on my saw is 12", so I'm able to cut boards that are 5" when standing up vertically against the fence. If your blade is smaller, you'll need narrower boards.

2. Cut the end of each board at a 30-degree angle, then lay them on the table so the long side is facing up.

3. Measure 6" from the outside angle of the cut side and mark it off on the edge closest to you. I also like to draw a small angle so I remember which way to cut. In this case, you will want to angle the cut toward the one you already made so they're pointed toward each other.

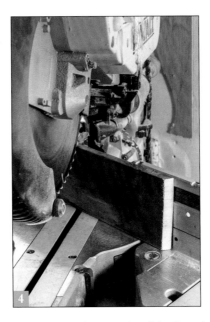

4. Stand the board up vertically. Cut on the outside of the line, then set the 6" piece aside.

5. Flip the remaining portion of the board over and repeat Steps 3 and 4.

6. Once you've cut six pieces, it's time to think about your desired finish. I opted to leave mine natural, so I sanded the boards really well with 100-grit sandpaper and an orbital sander. If you would like them rough, skip this step.

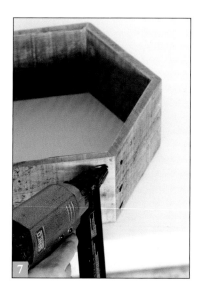

7. Apply glue on one of the angles and put two of the pieces together. Hold them together for about a minute, and then nail them together. Be sure to hold the nail gun straight on with the board you're nailing into so the nail doesn't pop through the side. Repeat this process with the remaining pieces until the hexagon is assembled.

8. If you'd like to paint or stain the shelf, now is the time to do so. I gave mine one final sanding with 220-grit sandpaper to make it nice and smooth.

9. Finally, attach a sawtooth hanger on the back, centering it on one of the sides, and your shelf is ready to hang.

CHICKEN WIRE MESSAGE BOARD

Another great project for using up scraps, the Chicken Wire Message Board is a simple but unique way to display notes, memos, and small trinkets. Chicken wire comes in several patterns and sizes, so feel free to choose whichever best fits your style. Small hooks or tiny clothespins work best for hanging items, and decorative thumbtacks look great stuck directly into the wood.

Tools

- Miter saw
- Wood glue
- Sandpaper
- Table saw
- Tin snips or pliers
- Hammer
- Thumbtacks or upholstery tacks

Materials

- At least eight pallet boards, 28" × 1¼"
- 22" × 13¼" piece of lauan or thin plywood
- 22" × 13¼" piece of chicken wire

Instructions

1. Cut the boards into several pieces, varying in length. Sand the pieces until smooth.

2. Sand the edges of the lauan or other plywood. Starting at the top left corner, begin to lay out the strips in a visually appealing pattern.

3. When you get to the right side, lay a piece in place and mark off where the edge of the plywood is. Cut with a miter saw. Repeat for the rest of the rows.

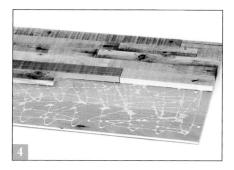

4. Once you have a pattern that you're happy with, tilt the plywood up and gently slide the boards forward onto the table, keeping the pattern intact. Spread glue all over the board and reassemble the pieces. Place something heavy on top and let dry.

5. Using the tip snips or pliers, cut a piece of chicken wire to fit the wood. Be sure to wear gloves, because the edges of the wire can be sharp.

6. If you wish to stain or seal the wood, do so now. I finished mine with a Light Brown wax, applying more to some spots to create a variety of colors. You may also spray-paint the chicken wire.

7. Attach each corner with a tack and then go all around the outside, adding as many as you wish.

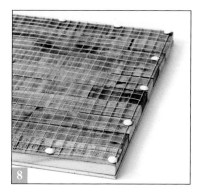

8. When everything is dry, lay the chicken wire over the top. Because it usually comes in a roll and will not lie perfectly straight, be sure to place it with the bend toward the ceiling so it's not tight against the board and there's room for hanging things once the wire is attached.

— FARMHOUSE WALL CLOCK —

I have to admit, I love vintage clocks. Every time I go to an antique store or an estate sale, I look for an old alarm clock to bring home and add to my collection. Needless to say, when I'm looking for a decorative piece for literally any room in the house, I always turn to a clock. They are timeless pieces (no pun intended) that will always have a use and can be found in a variety of styles and colors. Creating your own clock is a great way to personalize a space with a functional item that will never go out of style.

Tools

- Nail gun or hammer
- 1" nails
- Miter saw
- Wood glue
- Sandpaper
- Table saw
- Jigsaw or bandsaw
- Sharp #2 pencil
- String
- Thumbtack (optional)
- Drill or drill press
- ⅜" drill bit

Materials

- Pallet pieces (4): 15" × 3¾"
- Two 11" × 1½" × ¾" pieces (standard 1 × 2 from lumberyard)
- Clock movement kit made for ¾" surfaces

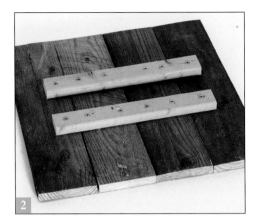

1. Lay out the four 15" boards so the edges are even. Place the clock mechanism in the center of the boards and trace around it.

2. Set the clock mechanism aside and take the two 11" pieces. Center them across the boards, placing one on the outside of each of the marks. Test fit the clock in the space, and then attach the two pieces with glue and nails.

3. Flip the piece over and use a tape measure to find the center. Drive in an extra nail just far enough to be sturdy, or push the thumbtack in place. Take a piece of string at least 12" long and tie it to the nail or thumbtack.

4. Pull the string out horizontally so it's almost at the edge of the board and tie it to the pencil. Keeping the string pulled tight, hold the pencil up straight and draw a circle around the center marker. Remove the nail or tack and set aside.

5. Use the jigsaw or bandsaw to cut out the circle.

6. Drill a hole in the center, using the ⅜" bit, to create a place to insert the clock. Test fit the clock mechanism and sand everything smooth, making sure the edges are even.

7. Paint the clock and set it aside to dry. Making sure the braces on the back are lying horizontally, divide the front up into 12 equal sections and paint the numbers on using a stencil, rub-on decal, freehand, or however you choose.

8. Once everything is dry, insert the clock mechanism and assemble according to the directions on the package. Attach a hook to the top back brace for hanging.

— PICTURE FRAME WALL ART —

Beautiful and customizable, this Picture Frame Wall Art can be created entirely from materials lying around the house. I based my design on a metal "Hello" I found at a craft store and chose three vintage wallpapers with floral designs that would highlight the gold word. Some other ideas include using patterned papers with kitchen designs and cardboard letters to spell out "Eat," using beach scrapbook paper and a cursive metal word that says "Relax," or using vintage pink-and-red wallpaper and wooden letters to say "Love." Use your imagination and get creative to make a piece that matches any room in your house.

Tools

- Miter saw
- Wood glue
- Sandpaper
- Spray mount
- Table saw
- Craft blade, such as X-Acto
- Hammer

Materials

- Picture frame
- 8 to 10 pallet boards
- Variety of wallpaper or scrapbook paper
- Decoration such as a wooden or metal word
- Small finishing nails, wire, or hooks

1. Measure the back of the picture frame where the glass would go. My dimensions were 18" by 14", so I cut nine boards that were 14" × 2", but you'll need to adjust the measurements based on your frame. Sand the pieces smooth.

2. Spray-paint the frame and set aside to dry.

3. Spray each piece with spray mount and wait about a minute until tacky. Lay a piece of paper over each board and rub it to smooth out any wrinkles and firmly attach it. Let dry.

4. Flip each board over so the paper is facing down and cut off the excess using the craft blade.
5. Flip the boards back over and sand the paper until it looks weathered and distressed.

6. Apply a bead of glue in the track of the picture frame where the glass would go. Insert each board, paper side down, alternating the patterns. Place a heavy object on top and let dry.

7. To finish, attach the decorative piece to the front of the frame. My metal "Hello" had two holes for nails, but you can use wire or hooks as appropriate.

TEALIGHT CANDLE HOLDERS

Simple and sweet, these Tealight Candle Holders are a great way to use up the extra-thick boards left over from other projects. Not only can they be customized to match any décor, but they make great gifts for even the hardest people to buy for on your list. Use an extra-long board with several candles to decorate a Thanksgiving tablescape, or a single tealight painted gold for a high-end accent in a living room. Use your imagination to create a unique piece, but as with any candle, please do not leave it to burn unattended.

Tools

- Drill or drill press
- 1½" paddle bit
- Miter saw
- Sandpaper

Materials

- Various lengths of the thick legs from a pallet
- Tealight candles
- Paint, wallpaper scraps, wax, etc., to decorate with

1. Begin by cutting various lengths of the pallet legs. Some ideas include pieces that are 4" long for a single tealight or 12" long to hold several to display on a dining room table. Sand them smooth.

2. Mark off on the board where you want the tealights, and use the paddle bit to drill straight down into the board about ½". Once you drill a few you'll be able to get a feel for how deep to drill so the tealight is flush with the top of the board. When starting out, it's easiest to drill down a bit and test the candle to see how it fits, and then drill again if needed.

3. Once all the holes are drilled, sand them inside and wipe away all of the dust.

4. To add some character, use the miter saw, for example, to cut the corners off or cut one side on an angle.

5. Finish the candle holders with stain or wax, painted accent sides, or wallpaper or scrapbook paper attached to the top with spray mount. Do not feel limited by these ideas, though—be creative!

CHAPTER SIX

FURNITURE

HANGING SHELF

These shelves are probably the easiest item to make from pallets, as they are nearly formed already when you get the pallet! They can be used in a variety of ways, such as bookshelves or picture displays.

Materials

- 6 – #6 × 1¼" multipurpose screws
- ³⁄₃₂" drill bit
- Reciprocating or jigsaw
- Sander with 60 grit paper
- Stain
- Electric drill

Instructions

1. When possible, use a pallet that you can get two shelves out of.

2. Mark out your desired height and cut the pallet with a reciprocating saw.

3. Cut off two extra boards for the bottoms of the shelves.

4. Sand off the rough edges.

5. Flip the shelf upside down to place the bottom board. Pre-drill the holes to avoid splitting the pallet wood with the screws.

6. Adhere the bottom piece with three multipurpose screws per shelf.

7. I stained mine and then sanded them again to give a weathered look.

END TABLE

This small table may look frail, but is quite sturdy once screwed all together. There are a lot of end tables out there for purchase, but this style is hard to find and makes it a great little addition to any room.

Materials

- 12 - #6 × 1¼" multipurpose screws
- ³⁄₃₂" drill bit
- Reciprocating or jigsaw
- Miter saw
- Sander with 60 grit paper
- Acrylic paint
- Stain
- Polyurethane
- Wood glue
- Electric drill
- Small nails

Instructions

1. Choose a large pallet, as you will be using most of it for the table. The table will look nicer if it is made from all the same wood.

2. Cut out the tabletop with a reciprocating saw.

3. Cut off the extra edges on bottom. This way you can have a spot under the top piece to slide in the legs and screw them into sides of open drawers.

4. From the remaining pallet, measure out pieces for the legs. I cut off the entire bottom section three boards high because it measured out perfectly for making two equal leg pieces.

5. Cut the wood in half.

6. You will only need one side of a pallet for the legs. Remove the other side with a saw.

7. Remove the top horizontal stringer support. Use the bottom horizontal stringer support as a place to rest the shelf.

8. Set up your table in a general way to measure the size of the shelf.

9. Use the remaining pallet wood to cut out the shelf boards.

10. Sand all of the pieces and assemble the boards for the shelf. I like to use thin support slats and glue them on the underside of shelf boards so they don't show too much.

11. After the glue dries, hammer in a couple of nails for extra support.

12. Rest the tabletop on another object so you can line up the leg piece to screw it into the side.

13. Use one multipurpose screw for the top of each leg board (three per side). Turn the table around and screw in the remaining leg piece on opposite side.

14. Pre-drill the holes into the lip of shelf to avoid splitting the boards with the screws.

15. Set the shelf onto the lip and screw in the shelf piece. Use three screws at each end of the shelf for a total of six on the entire shelf.

16. Paint the table with acrylic paint (in this case, bright red).

17. Finish the wood with a dark polyshade, which has stain and polyurethane. Wipe the surface with a clean cloth after applying so that the red still shows up.

18. This nice, bright piece makes the room a little more interesting!

BENCH

Although a pallet bench might not be the first choice in your room for seating, it is perfect for sitting a moment to take shoes off by the door, or for extra seating when hosting a large group of people. It is also lightweight and nice to have when you need to move around to accommodate guests in different parts of your home. If you would like to make it cozier, just throw a couple cushions on top and you are set!

Materials

- 24 - #6 × 1¼" multipurpose screws
- 4 - #6 × 2" multipurpose screws
- Reciprocating or jigsaw
- Miter saw
- Sander with 60 grit paper
- Electric drill
- Acrylic paint
- Stain
- Polyurethane

Instructions

1. Find the perfect pallet. If you are able to find a nice pallet like this close-boarded stringer, you will already have your bench top constructed and just need to sand and make a couple cuts to finish it off!

2. Using a reciprocating or jigsaw, cut the pallet in half, making sure you cut on the outside of the middle stringer board, leaving you with the top of your bench already nailed together on each side.

3. Turn the bench to the underside and remove the top and bottom deck boards to make room for the bench legs.

4. It is important to reattach underside boards because this is what keeps your bench stable. Screw them into new spots, closer to center with four 1¼" screws apiece.

5. Find solid stringer boards to cut four legs and two support boards.

6. Line up the bench legs to the underside corners and drill holes for the screws, starting with two on the side of the bench to screw in horizontally.

7. Drill two screws through the top of the bench down vertically, as well. You will need a total of four screws per leg for a total of eight 1¼" screws.

8. Cut two support boards that measure the width of the bench legs at each end.

9. Screw supports into legs with 2" screws, one at each end of support for a total of four screws.

10. This bench seems to be made for this spot. I painted it with white and then added definition to the edges of each board with dark stain. Finished with polyurethane.

BAR

A pallet bar can be used inside the home or outdoors. You can make them vertical for high stools or standing, or build them horizontally to be more table-like. Once assembled, they are very heavy and strenuous to move. If possible, I suggest assembling the piece where you will be using it. This tall bar is great for outside, when you want to take a break from gardening, or when barbecuing with friends.

Materials

- 6 large steel mending braces
- 52 - #6 × 1¼" multipurpose screws
- 20 - #6 × 2" screws
- Wood glue
- Reciprocating saw
- Miter saw
- Stain
- Polyurethane

Instructions

1. First, find two block pallets that match.

2. Use flat, smooth, solid pieces for the top of the bar as it will have to stand up to people leaning or resting their arms on it.

3. This is the frame for the top of the bar. It may be a hybrid pallet, but it can easily be crafted with four long stringer boards and two short boards for ends regardless. Use twenty 2" screws to assemble. Screw in six on each long stringer duo to secure, and four on each short board to screw down into long pieces.

4. Use the reciprocating saw to get the deck boards for your bar top. Sand smooth.

5. Now it is time to assemble the bar base. Lay one of your block pallets with the bottom deck boards facing up. Apply the wood glue.

6. You can use a generous amount, but keep in mind that the glue is just to help keep the pallets from moving when screwing in mending braces. The glue will not be strong enough to lift the base horizontally and keep it together.

7. Now take the second pallet and carefully place it on top, making sure the blocks are lined up so you can screw the braces in straight. Allow the glue to dry for thirty minutes.

8. Screw in the mending braces. The braces shown used six 1¼" screws each.

9. The deck boards will need supports to screw into, so cut two pieces to fit into frame at each end. Make sure you leave enough space between the supports to allow the bar top to fit over the bar base with block pallets sitting inside long stringer sides. You can glue these to the inside of the frame or just hammer them into place, as they will be secure once you screw deck boards into them.

10. Screw deck boards into vertical support boards and horizontal side stringers with ten 1¼" screws, two per board.

11. It is a good idea to use a countersink bit while pre-drilling the holes for the screws, so no screw heads will be sticking above the bar's surface.

12. Now, stand the bar base up and set the top of bar in place. Screw the bar top into the block of base if possible for tightest bond. Use six 1¼" screws (three per pallet), one for each block.

13. This bar was so heavy and awkward in my house, but I love it outside! For a style like this one, use a green stain, or another color of your choice, and finish with polyurethane. Paint the mending braces to give it a more finished look.

CHEST

Here is a sturdy piece of furniture that is timeless. With this project, it is very important to get all of the pieces aligned evenly so the top closes tightly. This chest usually takes the longest to make because of the small adjustments needed here and there, depending how straight or thick the deck boards you are using come out. With a little (or a lot of) patience, you can build this chest to any size you like and customize with a range of hinges and latches to accompany the look you are going for. I use this handsome piece for video game storage next to the TV, but it can also be used to hold small blankets next to the couch for cold nights, or even as a coffee table!

Materials

- 36 – #6 × 1¼" multipurpose screws
- 24 – #6 × ⅝" screws
- 6 L-brackets
- 2 – ½" metal hinges
- 1 metal latch
- Reciprocating saw
- Miter saw
- Electric drill
- Sander with 60 grit paper
- Stain

1. This project takes a lot of wood. Try to find the straightest boards you can, it
    will make this go so much easier.

2. These boards will be used for the sides and trim. I chose boards that differ
    slightly in color to add contrast.

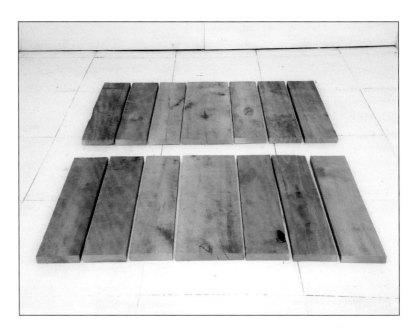

3. Make your cuts for the front and back panels. Use all the same boards by cutting them in half if possible so that the chest looks uniform. Sand the boards.

4. Make the cuts for the side panels. Sand the boards.

5. Cut four pieces of trim for the side panels, sand, and screw them on using 1¼" screws.

6. Glue two braces on the insides of the panels to hold them together. The reason behind this is you are going to want to line up the front and back panels to the sides before you get an exact measurement for how long to cut the trim for the front/back pieces as the trim will extend out, covering the side pieces.

7. Pre-drill the holes for the screws to make sure all of the screws go in nice and easy. Screw the side panels into the front and back panels.

8. Now that you have all four sides lined up, measure how long you will need to cut trim pieces. Sometimes at this point, the boards may have moved slightly. To avoid this, I recommend measuring step-by-step as the project progresses.

9. After making the cuts and sanding, glue your four pieces of trim on the front and back panels for extra support.

10. Drill the holes for the screws to attach the trim pieces into the side panel trim pieces.

11. Clamp and allow the pieces to dry for thirty minutes. Then screw in the front and back trim to the side trim.

12. Make the cut for the bottom pieces, sand, and fit them inside to see if you need to make any adjustments on size.

13. Fit inside and attach to lower side planks using L-brackets and $\frac{5}{8}$" screws.

14. Use two L-brackets per bottom board for a total of six.

15. Make cuts for the top piece, sand, and again fit on top to ensure that they cover the entire rim around the chest top.

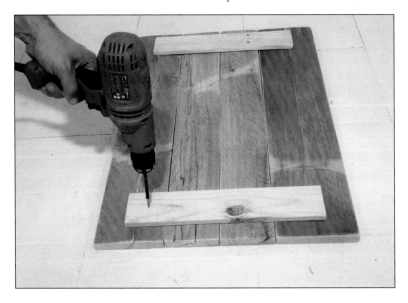

16. Cut two boards to keep top pieces together. Position them on the inside of the top boards in a way that they will just fit inside the chest when closed, so as to grab the sides and secure the chest shut.

17. Measure placements for the hinges on the back. There is more than one way to use the hinges; the one shown is the easiest method I have found.

18. Screw in the hinges. Most hinges will come with their own set of screws.

19. Measure the exact middle location for your latch.

20. Screw the latch into place.

21. It will have to line up with corresponding piece on the top plank. Like the hinges, the latches will come with screws in most cases.

22. You are done! Move the top up and down to see if you need to tighten up the hinges and ensure that the latch is correctly placed.

23. I like the wood to stand out on the chests, so I used a light-colored stain to bring out the darker parts of the wood and protect it from liquids or stains. This chest would look good anywhere!

HEADBOARD

Making your own headboard is a great way to save money and get exactly what you want. Bedroom sets can be rather expensive, especially if you are looking for something unique. This project is straightforward to do but can be cumbersome, so I would suggest either assembling it close to the room you will be using it in or planning on possibly breaking it down before moving it when it's complete. You can add hooks, lights, or use it for shelving to add functionality to your piece.

Materials

- 32 - #6 × 1¼" multipurpose screws
- 4 - #6 × 2" multipurpose screws
- Reciprocating or jigsaw
- Miter saw
- Sander with 60 grit paper
- Stain

Instructions

1. Find a large pallet to use as the framework. If you are making this for a queen-sized bed or larger, you will want long stringers. Many industrial companies will have extra pallets of this size.

2. For a queen-sized mattress, you will need multiple deck boards of at least 40" in length to assure you do not see where the boards end. It is not as necessary with this project to find boards that are exactly the same width, color, or look, so pick out whichever boards you like and sand them smooth.

3. You will need three stringers for the frame, two long deck boards for cross braces to screw the headboard planks into, and one more for the top trim.

4. Cut the stringer boards to your desired length with the miter saw. Screw three stringers together attaching horizontal stringer to vertical sides with two 2" screws at the top of each sideboard for a total of four screws.

5. Since the side frame stringers are only attached at the top, there will be a lot of movement, so make sure to cut your cross brace boards the same length as the top of your frame as it is now. When screwing both braces (especially the lowest cross brace), move the side stringers to your liking so that they hit your cross boards evenly. Screw in each brace board with four 1¼" screws, two on each end. You could also add one in the middle of the top cross brace to secure it to the frame.

6. Cut the top trim board, leaving extra length over each side to add embellishments. Sand the piece, and then screw in the trim with three 1¼" screws.

7. Arrange the headboard planks to your liking and screw each board into each
   cross brace with one screw in each spot. You will have a total of two 1¼"
   screws per plank.

8. Stand the headboard up to see if there are any unruly boards that need extra attention and to make sure the frame is solid.

9. I used three different shades of stain on the selected boards. I let it dry for a couple of days to make sure it was free of fumes before bringing it inside.

DECK CHAIR

It is not easy to find perfect pallets for deck chairs! Plan on reassembling most pallets an inch here and there so that they fit together just right. I ended up locating two that would work, but it took some driving around. This chair is a lounge-style and low to the ground. It's great for relaxing by the pool or around a fire pit.

Materials

- 12 - #6 × 1¼" multipurpose screws
- 10 - #6 × 2" multipurpose screws
- Reciprocating saw
- Miter saw
- Sander with 60 grit paper
- Electric drill
- Acrylic paint
- Stain
- Polyurethane

Instructions

1. Find similar sized pallets and extra boards for legs, supports, and trim. Your outside stringer boards on the backrest pallet will have to be slightly wider than those of the pallet you are using as the seat (or vise-versa) so that you can fit them in next to each other.

2. Remove boards on each pallet at the location where you will be joining them.

3. Set the seat piece on the floor and measure the width of the middle stringer board.

4. Remove enough of the middle stringer on the backrest pallet to allow room for two pallets to fit together.

5. Slide the pallets together to see if you have the right fit or need to make further adjustments to either piece.

6. Screw the backrest pallet into the seat pallet with four 2" screws, two on each side.

7. Cut two support pieces for the back of the chair.

8. Screw supports in at the top behind the backrest pallet, joining them to the seat pallet at the bottom with 1¼" screws. Use four per support board for a total of eight.

9. Using a reciprocating or jigsaw, cut off the end of the last bottom deck board piece on each side of the seat pallet to make room for the legs.

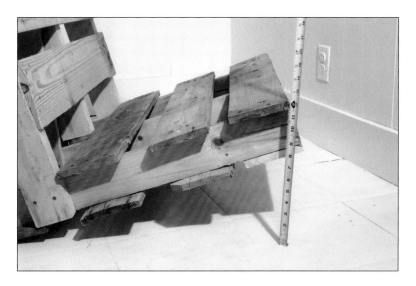

10. Lean the chair at the desired angle and then measure the outside height from the seat edge to the ground.

11. Also measure the inside height from the seat to the ground. Mark the leg board with both measurements, drawing a straight line between them. Make your cut with the miter saw and the outcome will be a leg piece with an angled cut at the top. Screw in the leg pieces with three 2" screws per piece for a total of six screws.

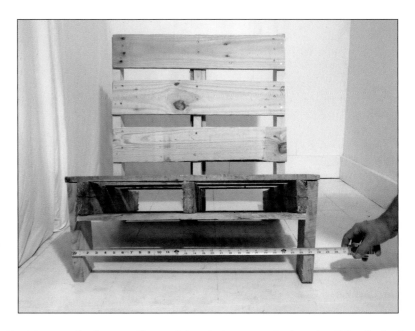

12. Measure the bottom front of the chair to get the length of the final trim piece, which will also add support.

13. Screw the trim into place with four 1¼" screws, two on each end.

14. Sand the chair to your liking. I left mine a little rough-looking everywhere except the area used for seating. I painted it mango, brushed dark stain over it, and wiped some off. Finished with polyurethane.

COFFEE TABLE

Coffee tables are one of the most used pieces of furniture in the home. You want to create one that is stylish and will last for a long time. These tables can be as easy or detailed as you have time and effort for. I made a very simple table and added metal embellishments that are functional in style but also add an industrial flair.

Materials

- 8 steel mending braces
- 48 – #6 × ⅝" screws
- Wood glue
- Reciprocating or jigsaw
- Miter saw
- Sander with 60 grit paper
- Acrylic paint
- Stain
- Polyurethane

Instructions

1. Find the perfect pallet. If you cannot find a close-boarded pallet you like to start with, you could also assemble the tabletop board-by-board with hand-picked deck boards. Attach them to stringer boards or blocks underneath to achieve a similar look to this.

2. Find equal blocks that you can disassemble from another pallet and that will sit flush with each other. Remove the blocks with reciprocating saw and sand.

3. Set up blocks in a desired position. When screwing in the mending braces, apply a generous amount of wood glue to help keep the tabletop in place.

4. After sanding the tabletop, set it on top of the blocks and make small adjustments. Your primary concern should be that the outer sides of the blocks line up evenly with the outer sides of the tabletop so you can evenly attach braces. Allow the glue to dry for thirty minutes.

5. Drill the holes for $\frac{5}{8}$" screws; sometimes the blocks can be very tough to screw into, so this makes it easier. Finally, screw in the mending braces in locations on each block that offer the best bond with the top to bottom. These braces require six screws per brace for a total of forty-eight screws.

6. I left the mending braces as-is because I like the combination of wood and metal. This table is very low and works well as a footrest, too! This table is painted a shade of aqua. I then rubbed dark stain over it using a rag, and finished it with polyurethane.

CHAPTER SEVEN

HOME ACCENTS

WALL-HANGING MASON JAR ORGANIZER

These jars come in handy for toiletries, kitchen items, treats for pets, and look especially lovely as flower vases! The clamps can seem tricky to attach, but once you get them on, these jars can handle a lot of wear and tear. Mason jars are cheap and can be found at most department, grocery, and hardware stores. I have found them at thrift stores for as little as ten cents!

Materials

- 3 mason jars
- 3 hose clamps
- 3 - #6 × ¾" multipurpose screws
- Reciprocating or jigsaw
- Miter saw
- Sander with 60 grit paper
- Phillips head screwdriver

Instructions

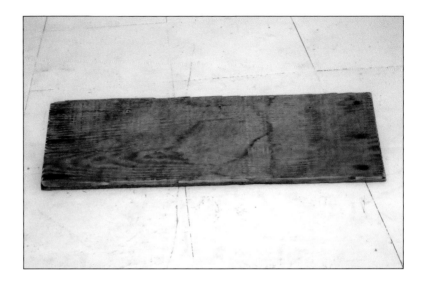

1. Use a board that is on the thicker side, at least ¾" thick. This sturdy backing is necessary for screwing in the hose clamps.

2. Choose the spacing for your clamps and pre-drill the holes for the screws.

3. This part can be a pain! I highly recommend using multipurpose screws. They go in the easiest, though you will need to put some effort into screwing the clamps on securely.

4. Screw in all three.

5. Hold jar at desired drop and tighten clamps with a Phillips head screwdriver.

6. The jars I chose were already shiny, so I left this piece natural with no finish to give it a rustic look. Hang the piece by screwing it directly into the wall because the jars are glass and will be handled frequently. If you anticipate filling the jars with heavy contents, I recommend screwing it into a stud in the wall.

PALLET-MOUNTED BOTTLE OPENER

This is a big hit with the guys! The pallet-mounted bottle opener is definitely one item that gets used more than any of the others I have made. There are so many different styles of wall-mountable bottle openers on the Internet, from different beer brewers to favorite sports teams, and all are relatively cheap. When mounting the piece, make sure that the wood is attached to the wall securely because of the pressure applied when used.

Materials

- Wall-mountable bottle opener
- Miter saw
- Sander with 60 grit paper
- Wood glue
- 2 - #6 × ⅝" screws
- Acrylic paint
- Polyurethane

Instructions

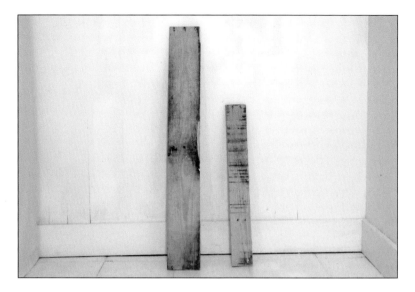

1. Use straight, even deck boards for your bottle opener. It will be held together by wood glue, so you will need the edges to meet together well.

2. Cut a piece as your backboard, making two cuts (the same width as the back board) for the bottom and the front of your cap catcher box. The two side cuts should be shorter. They should not be as wide as the front and bottom pieces because they will fit in between the back, front, and bottom boards.

3. Glue on the bottom and right side piece first so they can lean against each other.

4. Glue in the left side. Apply a layer of glue around the exposed rim where you will set the front piece.

5. Place the final piece.

6. Gently wipe off any excess glue.

7. Screw in the bottle opener with two ⅝" screws at the desired height.

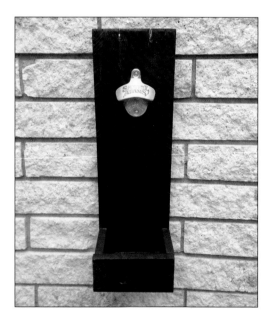

8. Paint the bottle opener with acrylic paint and cover with polyurethane to protect it from any spills. To make sure your bottle opener stands up to the pressure of repeated use, it is a good idea to try and find a stud to screw directly into instead of just hanging it on the wall. Screw the bottle opener into a secure section of wall to prevent damage from repeated use.

TOWEL RACK

If you think this just looks like a pallet shelf flipped upside down, you're right! In addition to functioning as a towel rack, this can also be used to hang toilet paper in the bathroom, or a paper towel holder or spice rack in the kitchen.

Materials

- $\frac{3}{32}$" drill bit
- $\frac{3}{4}$" spade drill bit
- 3 – #6 × 1$\frac{1}{4}$" multipurpose screws
- Reciprocating or jigsaw
- Sander with 60 grit paper
- Tension rod
- Stain
- Electric drill

Instructions

1. The length of the cut piece should account for the $\frac{3}{4}$" holes you will drill on each stringer board end.

2. Cut off an extra board for the top of the towel rack.

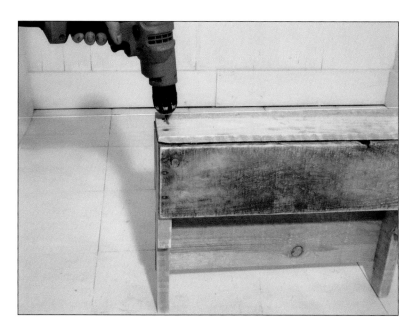

3. Sand the pieces, fit the extra board on top of the towel rack, and pre-drill holes for screws to prevent the pallet board from splitting.

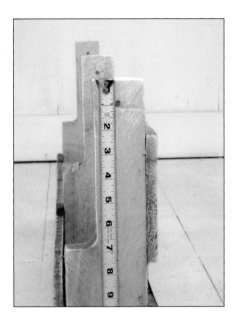

4. Screw in three multipurpose screws with an electric drill into the stringer board supports.

5. Measure and mark exactly where you want to drill holes for the tension rod.

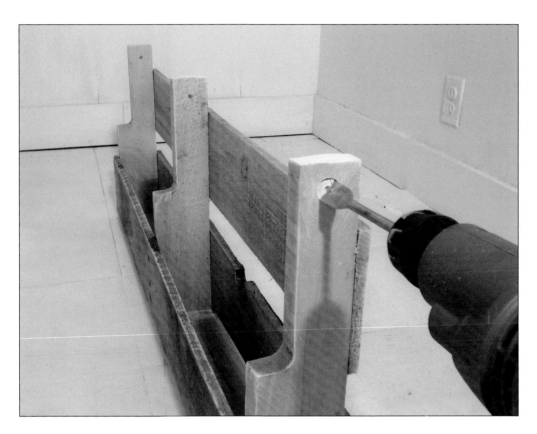

6. Use a spade drill bit to drill the holes. These drill bits require more strength than regular bits, so you'll need to put some muscle behind it.

7. After drilling the holes, sand them so there are no rough edges.

8. Finish the towel rack with a stain of your choice.

WALL-MOUNTED COAT RACK

There is a lot of room for creative expression with this one! Choose any kind of hook you have lying around or find in a store, placing as many or few as you like along the rack. For a more classic look, you may want to hold back on sanding after painting and use more ornate hooks.

Materials

- Reciprocating or jigsaw
- Sander with 60 grit paper
- Electric Drill
- 5 used/vintage metal hooks
- 10 – #6 × ⅝" screws
- Acrylic paint
- Spray paint
- Stain

Instructions

1. Measure the desired size according to how many hooks you are planning to use.

2. Select your desired hooks.

3. Position the hooks on the pallet to plan out spacing and screw into place. Alternatively, you can pre-drill the holes.

4. Remove the hardware and paint the rack.

5. Try using multiple shades of color at times to make the finish more interesting!

6. Notice the slight variations even though it is mostly the featured color you picked out.

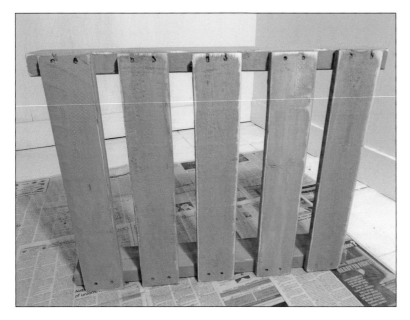

7. For a distressed look, lightly sand off some of the paint.

8. Apply the stain with polyurethane in it for shine.

9. Wipe the surface with a clean cloth, removing excess stain for a weathered look.

10. Notice the two boards on the right and the difference when stain is added.

11. Spray paint your hooks black, or another color of your choosing. Allow the wood to dry and screw them back into place. Using a small paintbrush, finish the screws with acrylic paint for a shinier finish.

12. Done and done! Hang the pallet using L–brackets that will stay hidden.

SCONCES

These sconces are so easy to make and would fit in almost any room and design scheme. I kept mine pretty simple, but there is much room for added detail. You can stencil behind the candle or use mod podge to transfer an image to the backboard. Just make sure to place the candle at a space and height far enough to keep the flame away from the image.

Materials

- Small nails
- Wood Glue
- Stain
- Miter Saw
- Reciprocating or jigsaw
- Sander with 60 grit paper

Instructions

1. Use a small pallet with wide boards to allow for a variety of candle sizes. This may seem daunting, but it's actually so easy to cut angled pieces with a miter saw. Simply swing the guide from 0 degrees all the way to the right to 45 degrees and cut.

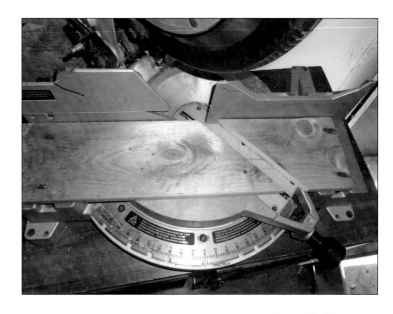

2. Bring the blade back to the original spot at 0 degrees. Slide the board back-wards so that the top of your angled cut is in the middle of the blade and make a straight cut down.

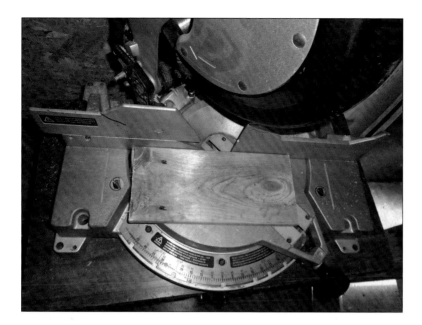

3. Set the triangle piece aside and make one more angled cut on the leftover piece of the board.

4. The result will be a matching triangle piece to make a set!

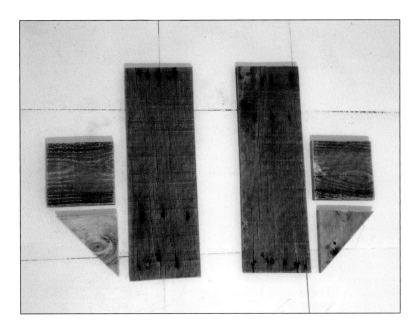

5. You now have all your pieces to assemble two sconces.

6. Glue your triangle piece first so you can best determine where to place the candle shelf.

7. Wipe off extra glue.

8. Glue on the candle shelf.

9. Allow the glue to dry for at least thirty minutes.

10. Hammer in some small nails for extra support.

11. Hammer diagonally into tip of triangle piece.

12. The stained gray offers a slight change, but not too different from the original look. The neutral background color is great for using candles of any color.

13. Just add candles!

DOOR HANDLE SERVING TRAY

This is the most popular item I have ever made. Although they are intended as serving trays, a lot of people use them purely as a display on coffee tables or kitchen counters, and some hang them on the wall as art. Using the type of handle that you can screw into from the top saves so much time and work. The only downside is that there is a much smaller variety of these types of handles as opposed to the kind you screw in from underneath the wood.

Materials

- 2 – ¼" black hammer pulls
- 8 – #6 × ¾" multipurpose screws
- Reciprocating or jigsaw
- Miter Saw
- Electric drill
- Sander with 60 grit paper
- Spray paint
- Polyurethane

1. Using three pallet boards, cut six pieces for the tray: four base boards and two for the handles. When making the trays, choose the best boards to make a flush, even tray. The individual boards often vary, so instead focus on the overall size of the tray you would like. However, the handle boards should match in size for aesthetic quality.

2. Push the boards together before assembling. This is helpful to get measurements before you make your cuts.

3. Make cuts with the miter saw and sand each piece. Flip the tray over and screw the baseboards into the bottoms of the handle boards. Make sure you screw deep enough that the screws don't stick out and scratch the surface of anything the tray may be placed on.

4. One screw on each end of baseboard is usually enough, but use more if needed.

5. Flip the tray right side up to examine for uneven pieces and to make sure the boards are screwed in straight.

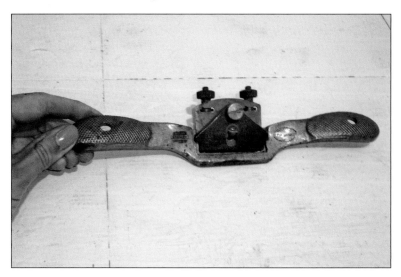

6. If you have any pieces that have rough edges and may cause a problem when setting glasses on the tray, you may be able to fix the problem by sanding it or possibly using a hand plane. These babies are awesome and come in quite handy!

7. I recommend using pulls that you can screw into from the top of the pull. There are a variety of handles out there you could use, but most have to be screwed in from the bottom of your board, as they are mostly used for cabinetry. I use these because trying to align those types of handles is a lot more work.

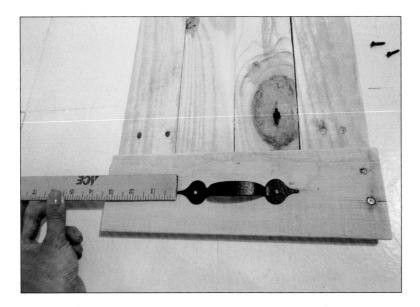

8. For this part, you want to be exact. Otherwise, you may end up grabbing the handles unevenly and possibly spilling the contents of the tray onto the unsuspecting guests you are serving!

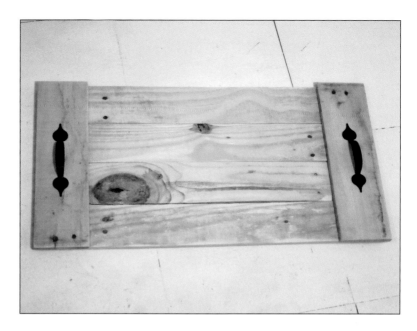

9. Measure and drill the holes into the boards. You can come back and screw the pulls into place once the tray is painted.

10. Lightly spray paint the tray in ivory. The light color allows you to see the wood and old nails still embedded in original pallet. Finish with polyurethane.

WINE RACK

This is a small-sized wine rack, but you can make them as wide as the pallet you use. Displaying your wine this way is inexpensive, attractive, and out of the way if you are hard-pressed for counter space. Cutting the holes in the bottom piece for hanging the glasses can be a learning process, but once you get a good one done, it may be helpful to save it as a guide for making glass holder boards in the future.

Materials

- 10 – #6 × 1¼" multipurpose screws
- Reciprocating or jigsaw
- Miter saw
- Sander with 60 grit paper
- Electric drill
- ¾" spade drill bit
- Dremel tool

Instructions

1. Choose a pallet that has the basic shape of the rack.

2. Using a reciprocating or jigsaw, cut the rack out of one corner of your pallet, making sure to include the outside and middle stringer boards so that the deck boards remain attached to them both. You will also need a board to wedge inside for the bottles to sit on and a bottom board that will hold the glasses.

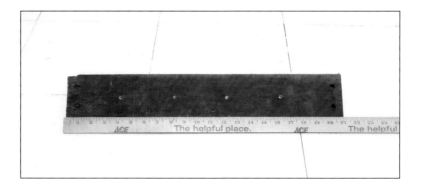

3. Measure out spots to drill holes for your wine glasses to hang from. In this example, the board is 21 inches long and you are going to make four holes for glasses. Divide 21 by 4 and you have 5.25. This will be the spacing for your marks, 5¼" apart.

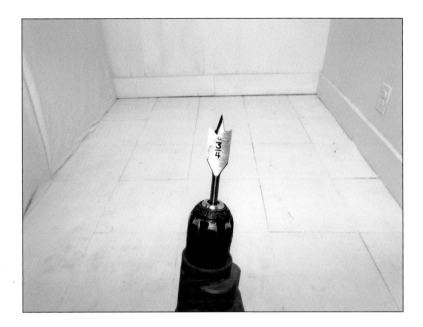

4. Use a ¾" spade drill bit to drill out holes. You will have to put some muscle behind it and make sure you hold the drill straight against the board.

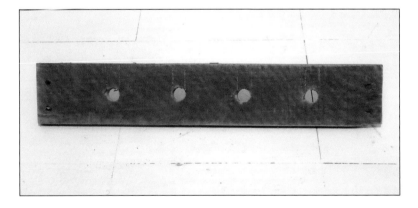

5. Yours holes should look fairly clean like the ones pictured, but if not, you can always go over them with a Dremel rotary tool. If you do not have one, sometimes you can get the job done with a jigsaw if you have a steady hand. Using a ruler, draw lines in pencil for your saw to follow to cut out remaining wood.

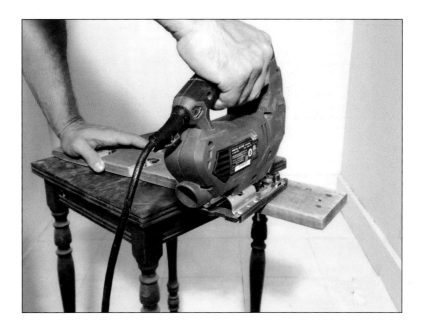

6. Cut out the wood using a jigsaw. You can also use a reciprocating saw by clamping the board to a workbench or a table to hold it securely.

7. The end result should look something like this!

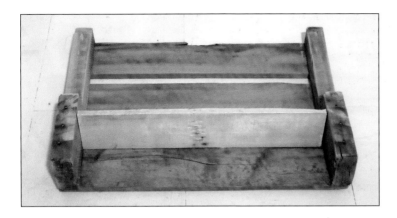

8. There are a couple of ways to get this middle board inside the wine rack. If it seems like the board is a close, tight fit, you can simply hammer it into place without taking the front board off. In this case, the front board was too long, blocking the glasses from sliding in and out with ease. It must be either shortened by trimming some of the wood off of the bottom while the board is still attached, or taken off and moved up a tiny amount. Since this board had room to be moved up, I went with the third option. While the front board is removed, place your board that sits inside in place.

9. Screw the front board back on, leaving enough space at the bottom for glasses to slide in, while also pinching the inside board and holding it secure. If you want extra support for the inside board, drill one hole on each side of the rack where the board sits. Follow it with one 1¼" screw in each side.

10. Flip the wine rack upside down and secure the bottom piece with four 1¼"
    screws, two on each end.

11. I left this piece looking rustic, only coating it with polyurethane.

CHAPTER EIGHT

DECOR

PALLET ARROW WALL ART

These arrows are fun to use in decorating your wall, as a nameplate for a child's bedroom, or to use outdoors to point guests in the right direction. They take about ten minutes to make and you only need one or two deck boards.

Materials

- Reciprocating or jigsaw
- Miter saw
- Wood glue
- Sander with 60 grit paper

Instructions

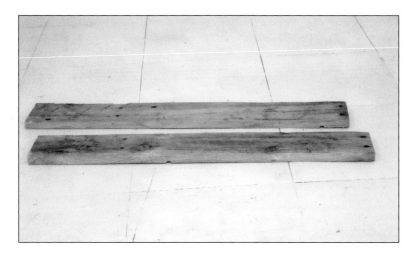

1. Use either one long board or two medium-sized boards depending on the size of arrow you want.

2. Place board on miter saw, "good" side up, and cut off the end at a 30-degree angle.

3. Flip your board over. Starting at the point of your previous cut, make another 30-degree cut.

4. This is the tip of your arrowhead.

5. Flip your board over to the "good" side again. Place the tip piece as a guide to where you will make your next cut, and then mark with a pencil.

6. Cut along the mark with a 30-degree angle.

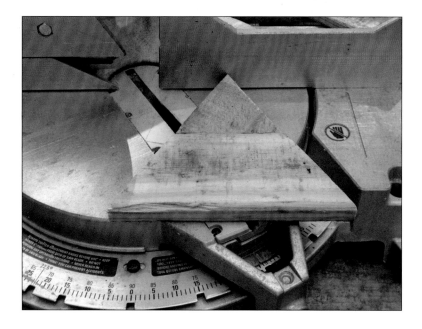

7. You have finished the arrowhead.

8. Turn your board around so you are dealing with the uncut end of the "good" side and cut off the end at a 45-degree angle.

9. Slide the board down to the desired length of the arrow feather and make another 45-degree cut.

10. Flip the board over and use the already cut arrow feather as a guide for the last feather piece. Cut the wood at a 45-degree angle.

11. You have finished the arrow feathers.

12. If you would like to add more detail, line up feathers even and make two more 45-degree cuts.

13. You now have all the pieces you need to assemble the arrow.

14. Glue the pieces on and allow the piece to dry for 30 minutes.

15. There are many ways to decorate these arrows, so have fun with it!

— PAINTED WALL ART —

If you search for pallet art on the Internet, you find a wide array of subjects and skill. Some crafters have specialized machines that help in making all those letters beautiful and straight, others are just that good at free hand. I have no machines and am not that good. I do have a printer though, and there is much you can do with just that! This project was so simple and worked on the first try, which is a rare experience for me with art projects!

Materials

- Wood glue
- Reciprocating or jigsaw
- Miter saw
- Sander with 60 grit paper
- Spray paint
- Cardstock
- Spray adhesive
- Acrylic paint
- Stain

Instructions

1. Use even, smooth boards, ideally from the same pallet that are light in color.

2. Make cuts to the desired size, along with two support boards. Sand the wood smooth.

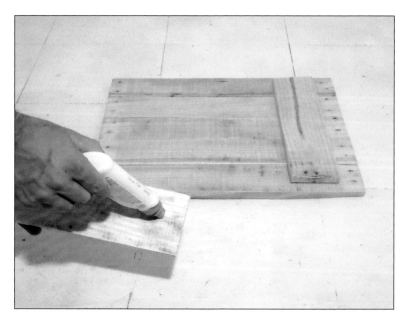

3. Glue the support boards on the backside of the boards so they stay hidden.

4. Allow the glue to dry for thirty minutes.

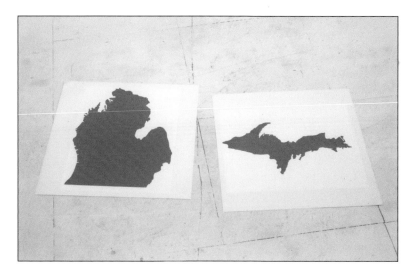

5. Print any image you like. There are many sites on the Internet that offer free printables. Make sure you download one large enough for the size project you have in mind. Silhouette prints work well for making your own stencil. Once printed, stick it onto a piece of cardstock paper with spray adhesive so you will have a sturdier stencil.

6. Cut out your stencil and arrange it to your liking on your pallet canvas. If you are having trouble keeping small pieces down on the boards, roll a small piece of Scotch tape and put it under the stencil to hold it in place.

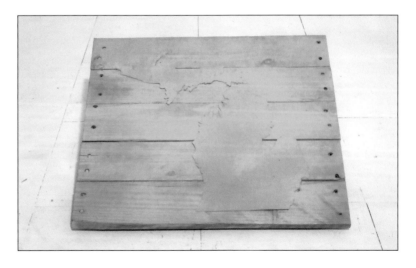

7. Using a can of spray paint, lay the board flat on the ground and completely cover the stencil and the board. Make sure you spray it with medium coverage; spraying on too much might cause drips that could seep under the stencil edges.

8. Wait for the paint to dry enough so that it will not smear, about ten minutes or so, and then remove the stencil.

9. Since this project is of my home state, I cut out a heart to place over the city I live in. Trace the heart and paint it any color.

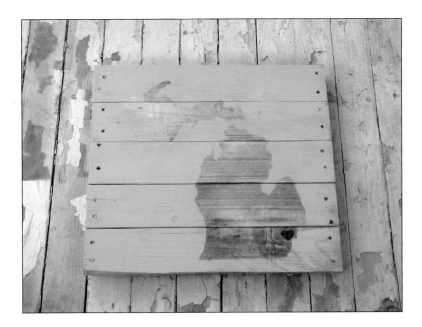

10. This project was much easier than expected, and I will definitely be doing more of this in the future. I sanded the heart to distress lightly and sealed the entire piece with a polyshade.

OUTDOOR FLOWER BOX

This flower box is basically a large pallet shelf, only not as tall. It is important to note how you assemble the bottom board so you can hold in dirt, but also still allow water to drain. If necessary, you can always drill tiny holes into the bottom board for water flow. Sealing this piece with polyurethane is a must if you want it to last.

Materials

- 4 – #6 × 1¼" multipurpose screws
- ³⁄₃₂" drill bit
- Reciprocating or jigsaw
- Electric drill
- Sander with 60 grit paper
- Stain

Instructions

1. Use a pallet that is long enough for the window where it will be hung.

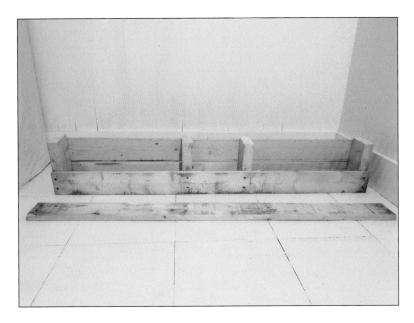

2. Cut off one end of pallet with the saw and an extra board to use as the bottom of the box.

3. Sand the pieces. Flip the box upside down and align the bottom piece to drill holes for screws.

4. Drill in four 1¼" screws so that there is one for each stringer board. The bottom board should fit on nice and tight, but with enough space for water to get through when watering plants. If you find that there is too much space between boards, you can use a plastic plant liner that will fit into the box unseen, or use wire screen to shape inside and hold the dirt in place.

5. Finished with a polyshade, which is stain plus polyurethane.

6. There is no standard for how to attach pallets to the outside of your home, though this flower box is attached to the underside of the window using L-brackets. You can also consider screwing it into the back board of the flower box, straight into the siding. Just do whatever works for you!

FLOWER ARRANGEMENT CENTERPIECE

These boxes can be used in so many ways! They are great for tables at weddings and parties but can also be useful as decorative mail holders or charger boxes for your devices. In this case, you can drill holes into the back board to allow cords to hang out and not get tangled. I use mine by the front door to throw keys and cell phones in so they are where I need them when I am ready to head out.

Materials

- 4 – 1½ × ⅝" corner iron brackets
- 14 – #6 × ⅝" screws
- Wood glue
- Miter Saw
- Reciprocating or jigsaw
- Sander with 60 grit paper
- Electric Drill
- Clamps
- Acrylic paint
- Stain
- 4 mason jars

Instructions

1. Using a couple of pallet boards, cut five pieces for the box.

2. Make cuts using a miter saw or whatever you have available that will cut straight.

3. Sand the pieces and arrange them so that the boards will support each other when you start gluing.

4. Start with a short end piece by applying wood glue to the sides and bottom of the board.

5. Continue gluing the remaining boards.

6. Clamp and allow the piece to dry for at least thirty minutes.

7. Once dried, screw in the L-brackets using $\frac{5}{8}$" screws on each corner for extra support.

8. Paint the piece in your desired colors. Fill the mason jars with water and flowers and place inside for a lovely display!

CLOTHESPIN PICTURE FRAME

The tricky part with making a pallet picture frame is always the glass. This frame is very simple to make, requires no glass, and is more accessible for switching out old pictures and updating your wall. You could use a variety of different clips to hang your photos or stencil designs on the edges of your frame.

Materials

- Wood clothespins
- Wood glue
- Reciprocating or jigsaw
- Miter saw
- Acrylic paint

Instructions

1. Cut the boards for the size of frame you would like, as well as two extra to hold it together.

2. Sand the wood smooth.

3. Place the boards next to each other and glue the support pieces on perpendicularly, either on front if you would like them to show, or hidden on the back.

4. Allow the glue to dry for thirty minutes.

5. Glue on the wooden clothespins at the desired height. Allow the glue to dry for thirty minutes before painting.

6. This frame has a "sketched" look to it that I achieved by painting it yellow and then brushing black over the cracks, edges, and clothespins with a tiny paintbrush.

ABOUT THE AUTHORS

Samantha Hartman is a graphic designer and self-taught woodworker with a passion for using reclaimed materials and salvaged wood in her designs. As the small business owner of Infinite Abyss, she was a finalist of Etsy Open Call in 2016 and has products sold in several shops throughout the country. Originally from Pittsburgh, she currently lives and creates in Wyoming.

Danny Darke is an amateur photographer and small business owner. She built Skid Row Palletes literally from the ground up, starting in her basement two years ago. When she isn't covered in stain, she is playing cards with her husband, Chris, and daughter, Frankie. Born and raised in the Metro-Detroit area where she still resides, she credits the spirit of Detroit for her hardworking attitude: "If you want something done, Do It Yourself!" You can visit her at skidrowpalletes.com.